New Heinemann Maths

Organising and Planning Guide

Heinemann is an imprint of Pearson Education Limited, a company incorporated in England and Wales, having its registered office at Edinburgh Gate, Harlow, Essex, CM20 2JE.
Registered company number: 872828

Heinemann is a registered trademark of Pearson Education Limited

Writing team

John T Blair

Percy W Farren

Myra A Pearson

Dorothy S Simpson

John W Thayers

David K Thomson

First published 2000

10
10

ISBN 9780435172046

Designed and illustrated by Gecko Limited, Bicester, Oxon.
Printed and bound in Great Britain by Ashford Colour Press, Gosport, Hants.

Acknowledgements
The objectives listed in the charts on pages 28–39 and 45 are from the National Numeracy Strategy publication *Framework for Teaching Mathematics from Reception to Year 6*, © Department for Education and Employment.

Contents

1 Introducing New Heinemann Maths

Mathematical development

New Heinemann Maths is a course designed to help teachers implement the content and teaching approaches described in the National Curriculum and the National Numeracy Strategy. Its clearly defined structure provides progression from Reception to Year 6 and offers schools a teaching programme with both coherence and continuity.

There is an emphasis on direct, interactive teaching aimed at helping children to develop a range of mental calculation strategies. These include the ability to recall basic facts quickly, calculate accurately with pencil and paper, use appropriate mathematical vocabulary and make connections between different areas of mathematics.

Effective teaching

Each mathematical topic in the *Teaching File* is developed systematically through a series of carefully structured lessons and linked *Pupil Activities*. The lessons provide the opportunity for direct, interactive teaching, and oral and mental work involving the whole class or a group on a daily basis.

Pupil Activities are provided to consolidate key teaching ideas and support group work, differentiation and discussion. Some of the small group activities require the children to work together in order to play a game or solve a problem. Suggestions on a range of simple and effective teaching resources to help motivate the children, illustrate a key teaching approach or enhance participation are included in each section of the *Teaching File*.

Classroom organisation

The components of **New Heinemann Maths** are designed for use in a flexible way. This ensures that the needs of children and teacher are met, whatever form of classroom organisation is used. Interactive *Teaching* activities can be used with a whole class or a large group. There are suitably differentiated *Pupil Activities* and written practice, consolidation, application and extension work in the *Textbook, Activity Book* and *Extension Textbook* designed for use with groups, individuals or the whole class. These can be used to allow the teacher to work uninterrupted with any children needing additional support.

Mental calculation

The course stresses the importance of children developing the ability to 'work things out in their heads'. There is, therefore, an emphasis on oral, mental mathematics, rapid random recall of basic number facts and children explaining their methods. To acquire the necessary skills and the confidence to do this, number facts and a range of mental calculation strategies are taught and practised in a systematic way. Children are encouraged to memorise these facts and to use mental strategies when they cannot recall them.

Planning for learning

Detailed advice and examples of long- and short-term plans are given on pages 17–20 of this *Organising and Planning Guide*. The emphasis is on creating a coherent and manageable form of planning that reflects the guidance given in the National Numeracy Strategy.

Assessment and recording

New Heinemann Maths provides a range of assessment materials designed to help the teacher build up a detailed picture of the children's attainment and to check that key objectives are being met. These materials complement the teacher's ongoing informal assessments, which are carried out on a daily basis by interacting with children or observing them at work. The assessment material may cover a short section of work in a *Check-up*, or a whole topic in a *Topic Assessment*, or provide an end-of-year *Round-up* where different areas of mathematics are assessed.

The materials can be used as part of the process of giving feedback to children and to remind them of the progress they have made. They also provide a comprehensive record of achievement that can be shared with parents and other teachers.

Involving parents

Home Activities can be used to support a school's commitment of actively involving parents in their child's learning. They provide a number of straightforward activities that give parents confidence in helping their child with mathematics. For the child, *Home Activities* provide opportunities for further practice and consolidation.

2 New Heinemann Maths components

NHM 3 consists of the following components.

For teachers: *Organising and Planning Guide*
Teaching File
Teaching Resource Book
Answer Book

For children: *Textbook*
Activity Book
Extension Textbook
Assessment Booklet (including *Check-ups, Topic Assessments* and *Round-ups*)
Pupil Sheets (included in the *Teaching Resource Book*)
Home Activities (included in the *Teaching Resource Book*)
Resource Sheets (included in the *Teaching Resource Book*).

Organising and Planning Guide

* The guide outlines:
  – the main features of the course
  – the component parts of **NHM 3**
  – relationships to the National Numeracy Strategy.

* It provides advice about:
  – planning to use the course effectively
  – organising resources
  – teaching lessons and follow-up work
  – assessing learning.

* Also included are:
  – charts to show the mathematical content of **NHM 2** and **NHM 3**
  – a mapping to the key objectives of the National Numeracy Strategy
  – a framework planner and topic planner for the year
  – an example of a weekly planner
  – pupil record charts
  – an assessment record grid
  – a class record sheet for the key objectives.

Teaching File

* The file contains:
  – a bank of *Starters and other mental activities* to supplement those included in lessons throughout the file
  – teaching notes giving suggestions for lessons, pupil activities, further teaching, the use of the *Textbook, Activity Book* and *Extension Textbook* pages, follow-up activities and assessment.

Starters and other mental activities

- The *Teaching File* has a bank of suggestions for oral mental activities. These are intended to promote a 'feel' for number, quick recall of number facts and the flexible use of mental calculation strategies. They are designed to be interactive, involving the teacher and the whole class, or a large group.

  Used as 'starters' at the beginning of lessons, the activities help to keep skills 'ticking over', even when the main teaching has moved to another topic. They can, however, be used at any time for practice or consolidation, as well as to check whether children are ready for the next step.

- Some of the activities are *generic*, providing a 'format' which can be adapted to suit different topics. The remainder are linked to *specific* topics. This activity relates to 'Finding $\frac{1}{10}$ of a number'.

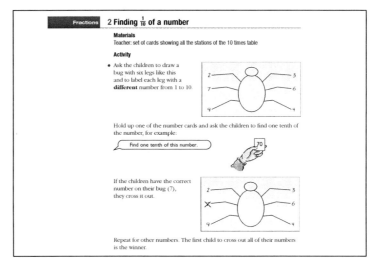

Teaching notes

- **NHM 3** includes the following mathematical topics:

Numbers to 1000, then 10 000	Money	Weight	Time
Addition to 100	Fractions	Length	3D Shape
Subtraction to 100	Addition and	Area	2D Shape
Multiplication	Subtraction to 1000	Capacity	Data Handling
Division			

- At the beginning of each topic a summary page provides:
    - a description of related *Previous work*
    - a concise *Overview* of the work of the new topic
    - a *Development* section, which details the mathematical content and suggested teaching approaches for the topic

– a *Contents* table containing references to teacher and pupil materials required for each section within the topic
– a *Language* list of relevant mathematical vocabulary
– a *Resources* list, which outlines general materials and specific *Resource Sheets*.

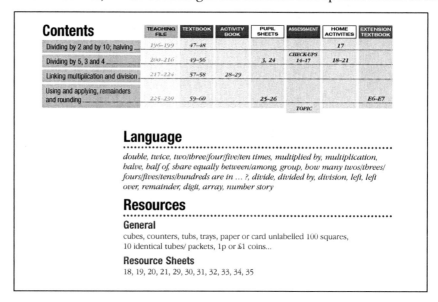

Contents

	TEACHING FILE	TEXTBOOK	ACTIVITY BOOK	PUPIL SHEETS	ASSESSMENT	HOME ACTIVITIES	EXTENSION TEXTBOOK
Dividing by 2 and by 10; halving	196–199	47–48				17	
Dividing by 5, 3 and 4	200–216	49–56		3, 24	CHECK-UPS 14–17	18–21	
Linking multiplication and division	217–224	57–58	28–29				
Using and applying, remainders and rounding	225–230	59–60		25–26			E6–E7
					TOPIC		

Language
....

double, twice, two/three/four/five/ten times, multiplied by, multiplication, halve, half of, share equally between/among, group, how many twos/threes/ fours/fives/tens/hundreds are in ... ?, divide, divided by, division, left, left over, remainder, digit, array, number story

Resources
....

General
cubes, counters, tubs, trays, paper or card unlabelled 100 squares, 10 identical tubes/ packets, 1p or £1 coins...

Resource Sheets
18, 19, 20, 21, 29, 30, 31, 32, 33, 34, 35

• The notes for each section within a topic follow the same pattern.

A brief statement outlines the work covered by the section.

A *Schematic* diagram details the lessons within the section. It shows how all the associated materials in **NHM 3** fit together and progress through the work of the section.

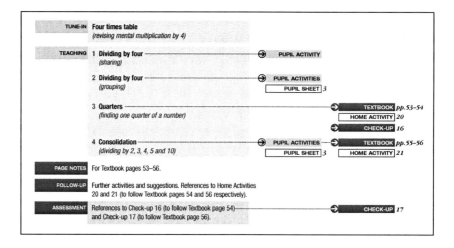

TUNE-IN

A *Tune-in* is then provided as a suggestion for starting the teaching. This is an interactive, mental, whole class activity which revises any relevant previous work and sets the scene for the first lesson of the section.

An activity from the bank of *Starters and other mental activities* can be used, if required, as a lead-in to subsequent lessons. Alternatively, an activity from the previous day's work can be adapted for this purpose.

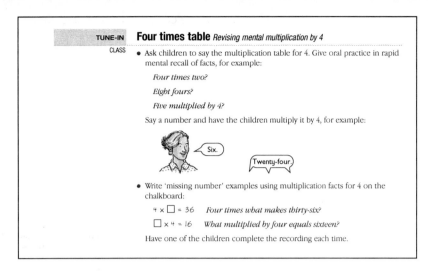

TEACHING

Teaching suggestions are given for class lessons to develop the sequence of work in the section.

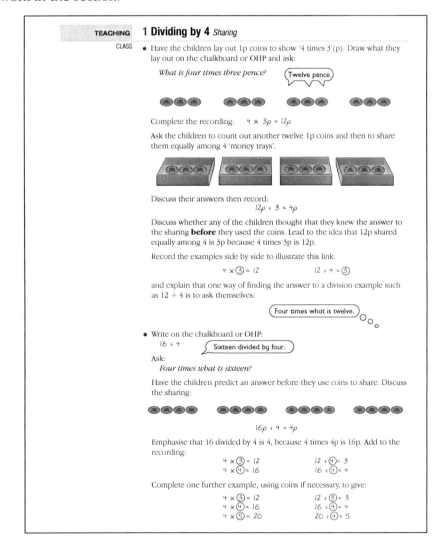

PUPIL ACTIVITIES

Pupil Activities, including practical activities, games and mental work, follow many of the lessons. These are designed to be used by groups, pairs or individuals, with some teacher support. When several activities are provided, a selection should be made to suit groups within the class.

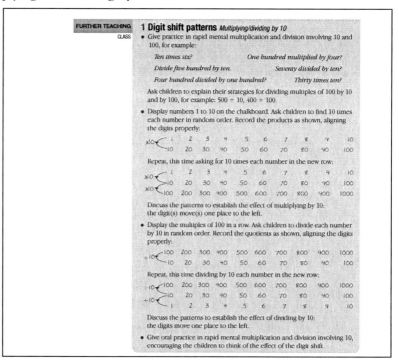

References to *Textbook* and/or *Activity Book* pages point to appropriate written work for pupils.

 **ACTIVITY BOOK**
Page 27

 **TEXTBOOK**
Page 44

FURTHER TEACHING

References are given to *Further Teaching*, if any.

 **FURTHER TEACHING**
1

Suggestions for *Further Teaching* lessons with the class or a group provide an alternative approach, consolidation or extension. The following consolidates multiplying and dividing by 10.

PAGE NOTES

Page Notes offer advice about using some of the relevant *Textbook* and *Activity Book* pages. The notes highlight more challenging examples and possible difficulties with language and instructions.

FOLLOW-UP

Follow-up suggestions are given for drawing lessons to a close. These often involve whole class discussion, mental work, extension activities or further practice.

References are also given to:
– *Home Activities* related to the *Textbook* and *Activity Book* pages.

The Assessment section may include:
- a reference to a *Check-up* associated with the work of the section
- page notes for *Topic Assessments*.

The *Topic Assessments* are designed to assess a number, money or time topic, covering the work of several sections. The notes point out some common errors that may occur and make some suggestions for dealing with them. For each question there are references to relevant *Textbook* or *Activity Book* pages and the appropriate section of the *Teaching File*, should some re-teaching or additional practice be required.

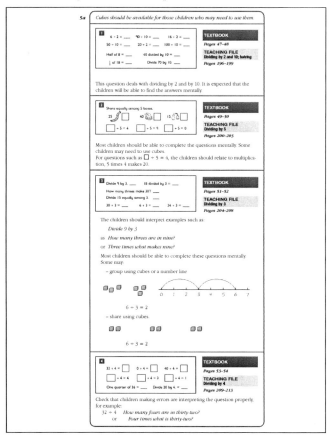

Teaching Resource Book

- The book contains:
  - photocopiable *Pupil Sheets* for use either within a lesson or as follow-up practice, consolidation or extension
  - photocopiable *Home Activities* to give homework linked to the work in school
  - photocopiable *Resource Sheets* for use by the teacher during lessons.

Pupil Sheets

- The **NHM 3** *Teaching Resource Book* includes 54 photocopiable *Pupil Sheets*. There are several types which have different purposes. For example:
  - to provide a means of recording during the course of a lesson
  - to give extra practice to children who have completed the *Textbook* or *Activity Book* pages but need more examples
  - to provide a template for teachers to produce their own sheets, which can be customised to cater for different ability levels.

Home Activities

- The **NHM 3** *Teaching Resource Book* contains 27 *Home Activities* and 4 *Home Sheets* of associated 'cards' for use with some of them. These are photocopiable.

The activities aim to:
  – provide important extra practice for the child
  – give parents an opportunity to be actively involved with their child's learning and provide encouragement and help
  – inform those at home about the mathematics being taught in school.

- *Home Activities* are referenced from:
  – the foot of the *Textbook* or *Activity Book* page which completes this work in school
  – the *Follow-up* section in the *Teaching File* for the related *Textbook* or *Activity Book* page.

- There are two types of *Home Activity*:
  – simple oral, mental activities or games involving an adult and the child. There are straight-forward instructions for the adult which give examples of the language to be used
  – written practice examples for the child to complete and the adult to check.

Often both types appear on one sheet. However, it is not necessary to use both parts at the same time.

Resource Sheets

- The **NHM3** *Teaching Resource Book* includes 53 photocopiable *Resource Sheets* for producing materials such as flashcards, number cards, 100-squares and so on, for use when teaching lessons.

Textbook and Activity Book

- **NHM 3** contains:
  – a Textbook
  – an Activity Book

- The *Textbook* and *Activity Book* contain written work for the children for use after the *Teaching* of a lesson and related *Pupil Activities* have been completed. The pages provide practice, consolidation and application.

This page follows the *Teaching* about 'Dividing by 3'.

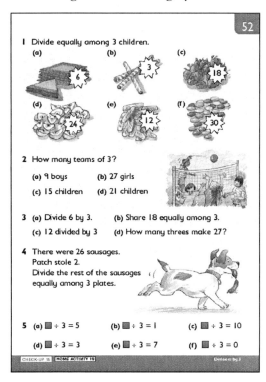

- There are references at the foot of some of the *Textbook* and *Activity Book* pages to:
  - *Check-ups*, which assess one or two sections of work
  - *Home Activities*, which provide related work for a child and adult at home
  - *Topic Assessments*, which assess the work related to a specific number, money or time topic.

Extension Textbook

- The *Extension Textbook* includes a range of activities to provide both lateral and vertical extension. The activities include mixed operations, 'multiple step' operations and mixed measures. Throughout the book children are encouraged to use and apply their knowledge and skills.

This page follows the core work on *Subtraction to 100*.

Assessment Book

- The *Assessment* book includes:
  - *Check-ups*
  - *Topic Assessments*
  - *Round-ups.*

- It is designed to assess children's understanding, knowledge and ability to apply skills and techniques. The assessments are provided in both booklet and photocopy master format. The **NHM 3** *Assessment Book* contains:
  - 27 *Check-ups* covering the topics shown:

Numbers to 1000	– 3	Money	– 2
Addition to 100	– 3	Fractions	– 2
Subtraction to 100	– 4	Addition and Subtraction to 1000	– 3
Multiplication	– 4	Time	– 3
Division	– 4		

  - 9 *Topic Assessments* covering:

Numbers to 1000	Multiplication	Money
Addition to 100	Division	Fractions
Subtraction to 100	Addition and Subtraction to 1000	Time

  - 3 *Round-ups* containing questions on number, money, shape, measure and data handling.

- Each *Check-up* covers a smaller range of work within a single topic and is linked to the work of several *Textbook* and *Activity Book* pages. One of the *Check-ups* for Division is shown below.

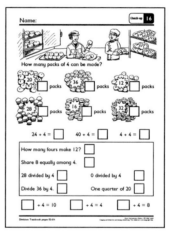

References to *Check-ups* are given in the *Teaching File* and at the foot of appropriate *Textbook* or *Activity Book* pages.

- The *Topic Assessments* cover work related to a whole topic. References to *Topic Assessments* are given in the *Teaching File*, at the end of the appropriate section of notes, and at the foot of the appropriate *Textbook* or *Activity Book* pages.

- The *Round-ups* are end-of-year tests which cover a wide range of 'mixed' mathematics. They give an indication of overall level of attainment for the year.

Answer Book

- The *Answer Book* contains answers for the:
  - *Activity Book*
  - *Textbook*
  - *Extension Textbook*
  - *Assessment*
  - *Home Activities.*

3 Using New Heinemann Maths

Learning and teaching

The approach to learning and teaching in **NHM 3** is based on the following key ideas:
- daily mathematics lessons
- direct, interactive teaching
- systematic development of mental calculation.

Given this approach, the *Teaching File* is a crucial component of **NHM 3**, as it provides guidance on:
- the development of each mathematical topic in a clear, systematic way
- teaching, pupil activities and follow-up work to promote understanding and develop and apply skills
- the effective use of resources to develop knowledge and understanding of key aspects of number work
- the use of mental and oral activities to develop and practise mental strategies and techniques.

Direct teaching is essential. It cannot be replaced by the use of *Pupil Sheets*, *Textbook* and other course materials. The function of such materials is to:
- check the children's understanding of what has been taught
- provide a record of work completed
- set new challenges where the children can apply the mathematics they have learned.

The **NHM 3** pupil materials are **not** designed to teach new concepts to children working through them on their own, without prior teaching and discussion. The focus is very much on direct teaching and interaction.

Direct teaching and interaction

High quality direct teaching and interaction are at the heart of both the National Numeracy Strategy and **New Heinemann Maths**. This two-way process encourages both teachers and children to be actively engaged in the learning process.

Children are expected to:
- be actively involved in answering questions
- contribute to discussion during *Teaching* activities and *Follow-up* discussions
- be able to explain and demonstrate understanding of their learning to others.

The *Teaching File* makes suggestions which enable the teacher to provide an effective direct teaching approach through an appropriate balance of the following methods.

Demonstration – showing and illustrating mathematics using appropriate resources and visual materials.

Teaching File, page 40
Numbers to 1000

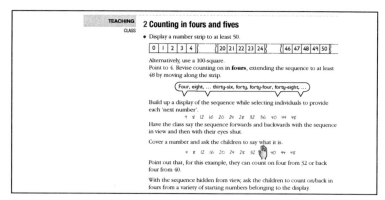

Instruction – giving information clearly and precisely.

Teaching File, page 92
Addition to 100

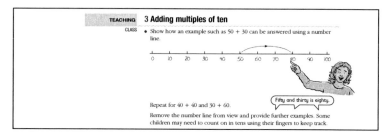

Direction – sharing teaching objectives with the children and making sure they know what they should be learning.

Teaching File, page 338
Capacity

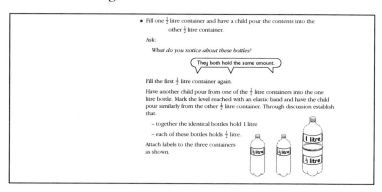

Explanation and illustration – giving accurate, well-paced explanations.

Teaching File, page 221
Division

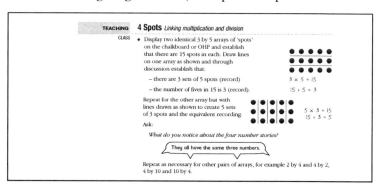

Questioning – using effective questioning techniques to:
- ensure that children are actively involved in their learning
- encourage the children to explain what they are doing
- help the children to consider other possibile strategies and methods
- focus the children's attention on new aspects of their learning.

A wide range of open and closed questions is suggested within the *Teaching* activities in **NHM 3**.

Consolidating – maximising opportunities to reinforce and develop what has been taught through the use of:
- *Starters and other mental activities* to consolidate previous learning
- well-focused *Pupil Activities* and *Pupil Sheets*
- practice and applications in the *Textbook* and *Activity Book*
- *Extension* activities in the *Extension Textbook*.

Discussion and evaluation of children's responses – identifying mistakes and misunderstandings by using:
- oral *Follow-up* activities from the *Teaching File*
- *Check-ups* and *Topic Assessments* in the *Assessment* booklet.

This process can help to identify appropriate further teaching.

Summarising – reviewing with the children what has been taught and what the children have learned using:
- *Follow-up* activities.

Differentiation

The National Numeracy Strategy states that the children should, as far as possible, work together through the year's programme described in the Framework. **New Heinemann Maths** has also been designed to be used in this way. However, there will be times when the teacher wishes to work with groups of children or individual children. The *Teaching* activities in the *Teaching File* have been written for whole class teaching, but can be adapted for use with groups or individuals.

The following features of **NHM 3** can help the teacher to plan differentiated programmes:
- the ability to select from the suggested *Teaching* activities and *Pupil Activities* for each section in the *Teaching File* allows the teacher to plan appropriate programmes to match the children's needs
- *Pupil Sheets* provide further practice for those who need it. Some of them provide templates for teachers to customise for use with groups or individuals
- the activities within the *Extension Textbook* provide both lateral and vertical extension. They provide opportunities to extend children's thinking and learning.

The teacher should omit pages, parts of pages or questions in the *Textbook* or *Activity Book* which are not appropriate for specific children. However, all children should have experience of using and applying the mathematics they are learning.

Planning

Starting points
Planning for effective learning involves thinking about:

- the National Numeracy Strategy.
  The chart on pages 28–33 summarises the curriculum coverage provided by **NHM 3**.

- the children's previous experience in mathematics.
  This can be found by consulting:
  - the children's records of achievement
  - the mathematical development chart on pages 40–43.

- the development of the children's knowledge, skills and understanding.

Information relating to the work contained in **NHM 3** is found in:
- the pupil record grids on pages 46–47 of this guide
- the summary at the beginning of each new topic in the *Teaching File*. It describes *Previous work* and gives an *Overview* and a detailed *Development* of the topic. The *Contents* table lists the sections within the topic and all the **NHM 3** materials associated with them. The *Language* list gives a clear indication of the vocabulary used.

While there are many ways to plan a mathematics programme and schools will have their own planning formats, **NHM 3** provides examples of two types of year/term planner and one weekly planner. These are designed to provide a route through the materials. Year/term planners can be described in two ways: a 'framework planner' and a 'topic planner'.

Framework planner

The framework planner identifies each unit of work within the National Numeracy Strategy in order, and the objectives that are being addressed. This is then matched to the appropriate sections of **NHM 3**.

Detailed autumn, spring and summer planners are included on pages 28–33 of this guide.

7 Appendices

Appendix A: NHM 3 Framework planner   **Year 3: Autumn Term**

Unit	Framework Topic	Objectives: children will be taught to ...	NHM Topic	NHM Section	Teaching File pages	Date/comments
1	Place value, ordering, estimating, rounding Reading numbers from scales	• Read and write whole numbers to 1000 in figures and words. • Read and begin to write the vocabulary of comparing and ordering numbers. • Say the number that is 1, 10 or 100 more or less than any given two- or three-digit number.	Numbers to 1000	• **The sequence to 1000:** – uses the language: 'the number after/before/between', 'the number one or two more/less' – extends the number sequence to 1000 – introduces finding numbers 10 or 100 more/less – introduces adding/subtracting 10, 100, multiples of 10, multiples of 100. • **Number names, ordinal numbers:** – introduces number names for multiples of ten and multiples of one hundred.	43–54 73–78	
2–3	Understanding + and – Mental calculation strategies (+ and –) Money and 'real life' problems Making decisions and checking results	• Extend understanding of the operations of addition and subtraction, read and begin to write the related vocabulary, and continue to recognise that addition can be done in any order. Use the +, – and = signs. • **Know by heart:** **all addition and subtraction facts for each number to 20.** • Solve word problems involving numbers in 'real life', money and measures, using one or more steps, including finding totals and giving change, and working out which coins to pay. Explain how the problem was solved. • Recognise all coins and notes. **Understand and use £. p notation** (for example, know that £3·06 is £3 and 6p).	Addition to 100 Subtraction to 100 Money	• **Addition facts to 20:** – revises and consolidates addition facts to 20, for example, 6 + 8, 10 + 7 – systematises addition of a single digit and a teens number not bridging 20, for example, 15 + 3, 7 + 12. • **Consolidation of facts to 20:** – consolidates subtraction facts to 20. • **Using £1 and £2 coins:** – revises work with coin collections involving 1p, 2p, 5p, 10p, 50p and £1 coins – introduces the £2 coin – deals with converting amounts in pounds and pence to pence and vice-versa – includes finding change from £1 and £2 – involves finding the difference between two amounts.	84–89 120–125 236–243	
4–6	Measure, including problems Shape and Space Reasoning about shapes	• Read and begin to write the vocabulary related to length. Measure and compare using standard units (km, m, cm) including using a ruler to draw and measure lines to nearest half centimetre. Know the relationships between kilometres and metres, metres and centimetres. Begin to use decimal notation for metres and centimetres. • Suggest suitable units and measuring equipment to estimate or measure length. • Read scales to the nearest division (labelled or unlabelled). • Record estimates and measurements to the nearest whole or half unit (e.g. 'about 1·5 m'), or in mixed units (e.g. '3 m and 20 cm'). • Classify and describe 3-D and 2-D shapes, including the hemi-sphere, prism, semi-circle, quadrilateral ... referring to properties such as reflective symmetry (2-D), the number or shapes of faces, the number of sides/edges and vertices, whether sides/edges are the same length, whether or not angles are right angles ... • Make and describe shapes and patterns. Relate solid shapes to pictures of them.	Length 2D Shape 3D Shape	• **Length:** – introduces estimating and measuring lengths to the nearest half metre – revises measuring in metres and in centimetres and use of the abbreviation cm – introduces measuring and drawing lengths to the nearest half centimetre – introduces measuring using a tape measure – introduces measuring in metres and centimetres, for example, 2m 30cm. • **2D Shape: making shapes:** – deals with making quadrilaterals, pentagons, hexagons and octagons using triangles, rectangles and squares – uses composite shapes to copy, continue and create patterns. • **3D Shape:** – revises recognising and naming spheres, cubes, cuboids, cones, cylinders and pyramids from pictures and by handling solids – introduces prisms – deals with properties associated with these shape – faces, edges, vertices.	321–329 384–388 376–381	
7	Assess and review					

Topic planner

This planner takes an alternative approach by illustrating a progression in the teaching of each maths topic and matching the numeracy objectives to it. Each term has been subdivided into the same number of units as the framework planner.

Detailed autumn, spring and summer planners are included on pages 34–39 of this guide.

Unit	NHM Topic	NHM Section	Teaching File pages	Framework Topic	Objectives: children will be taught to ...	Date/comments
1–4	Numbers to 1000	• **Counting in twos, threes, fours and fives:** – revises and extends counting in twos, threes, fours and fives – revises and extends odd and even numbers.	38–42	Counting, properties of numbers and number sequences	• Count larger collections by grouping them: for example, in tens, then other numbers. • Describe and extend number sequences: **count on or back in ones or tens, starting from any two- or three-digit number;** count on or back in tens or hundreds, starting from any two- or three-digit number, and recognise odd and even numbers to at least 100; count on in steps of 3, 4 or 5 from any small number to at least 50, then back again.	
		• **The sequence to 1000:** – uses the language: 'the number after/before/between', 'the number one or two more/less' – extends the number sequence to 1000 – introduces finding numbers 10 or 100 more/less – introduces adding/subtracting 10, 100, multiples of 10, multiples of 100.	43–54			
		• **Counting in hundreds, tens and ones:** – deals with counting in hundreds, then in tens, then in ones to 1000.	55–57	Place value and ordering	• **Read and write whole numbers to at least 1000** in figures and words. • **Know what each digit represents,** and partition three-digit numbers into a multiple of 100, a multiple of ten and ones (HTU). • Read and begin to write the vocabulary of comparing and ordering numbers, including ordinal numbers to at least 100. Compare two given three-digit numbers, say which is more or less, and give a number which lies between them.	
		• **Place value, comparing and ordering:** – introduces place value for 3-digit numbers – deals with recognising – the largest/smaller number in a pair – the largest/smallest number in sets of up to six. – includes ordering up to six non-consecutive numbers, starting with the smallest/largest.	58–64		• Say the number that is 1, 10 or 100 more or less than any given two- or three-digit number. • **Order whole numbers to at least 1000,** and position them on a number line.	
		• **Numbers halfway between, estimating and rounding:** – deals with numbers halfway between two given numbers – develops ideas about estimation of a number from its position on a number line – consolidates rounding to the nearest ten and introduces rounding to the nearest hundred.	65–72	Estimating and rounding	• Read and begin to write the vocabulary of estimation and approximation. • Give a sensible estimate of up to about 100 objects. • Round any two-digit number to the nearest 10 and any three-digit number to the nearest 100. • Solve mathematical problems or puzzles, recognise simple patterns and relationships, generalise and predict. Suggest extensions by asking 'What if...?' • Investigate a general statement about familiar numbers by finding examples that satisfy it. • **Explain methods and reasoning** orally and, where appropriate, in writing.	
		• **Number names, ordinal numbers:** – introduces number names for multiples of ten and multiples of one hundred – consolidates first second, ... tenth and the notation 1st, 2nd, ... 10th – introduces eleventh, twelfth, ... twentieth and the notation 11th, 12th, ... 20th	73–78			
5	Length	• **Length:** – introduces estimating and measuring lengths to the nearest half metre – revises measuring in metres and in centimetres and the use of the abbreviation cm – introduces measuring and drawing lengths to the nearest half centimetre – introduces measuring using a tape measure – introduces measuring in metres and centimetres, for example, 2m 30cm.	321–329	Measures, including problems	• Read and begin to write the vocabulary related to length. • Measure and compare using standard units (km, m, cm), including using a ruler to draw and measure lines to the nearest half centimetre. Know the relationships between kilometres and metres, metres and centimetres. • Begin to use decimal notation for metres and centimetres. • Suggest suitable units and measuring equipment to estimate or measure length. • Read scales to the nearest division (labelled or unlabelled). • Record estimates and measurements to the nearest whole or half unit (e.g. 'about 1.5 m'), or in mixed units (e.g. '3 m and 20 cm').	
6	2D Shape	• **Making shapes:** – deals with making quadrilaterals, pentagons, hexagons and octagons using triangles, rectangles and squares – uses composite shapes to copy, continue and create patterns.	384–388	Shape and space Reasoning about shapes	• Classify and describe 2-D shapes, including the semi-circle, quadrilateral ... referring to properties such as reflective symmetry (2-D), the number or shapes of faces, the number of sides/edges and vertices, whether sides/edges are the same length, whether or not angles are right angles ... • Make and describe shapes and patterns: for example, explore the different shapes that can be made from four cubes. Relate solid shapes to pictures of them.	
		• **Position, movement and angle:** – revises turning clockwise and anticlockwise through whole, half and quarter turns – revises and extends the work on right angles – introduces grid references introduces the four compass directions North, South, East and West – revises moving forwards, turning left and right on a square grid introduces the abbreviations F, R and L.	389–396		• Read and begin to write the vocabulary related to position, direction and movement: for example, describe and find the position of a square on a grid of squares with the rows and columns labeled. Recognise and use the four compass directions N, S, E, W • Make and describe right-angled turns, including turns between the four compass points. • **Identify right angles** in 2-D shapes and the environment. Recognise that a straight line is equivalent to two right angles. Compare angles with a right angle.	
7	Assess and review			Assess and review		

Weekly planner

It is often necessary to plan in more detail on a weekly or daily basis. Plans of this type provide an indication of what the teacher hopes to cover during the course of the week. However, given that the mathematics must necessarily build on the needs of the children, an element of flexibility should be built in. This allows for modification to the plan as it is implemented.

The *Schematic* diagrams at the beginning of each section in the *Teaching File* provide a helpful starting point for this process.

Teaching File, page 261
Fractions

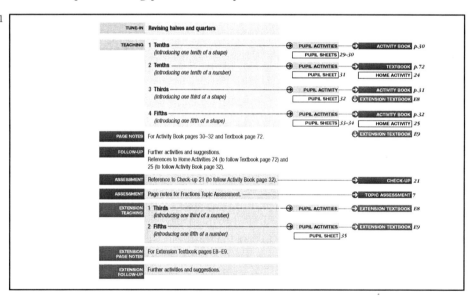

The weekly planner on page 20 shows how two sections of *Fractions* might be developed over the course of a week.

Weekly Planner: Tenths, thirds, fifths

SECTION	Tenths		Thirds	Fifths	
	Monday	**Tuesday**	**Wednesday**	**Thursday**	**Friday**
TUNE-IN or STARTER	**Tune-in** **Revising halves and quarters**	Activity from *Starters and other mental activities* related to 10 times table	Activity from *Starters and other mental activities* related to 3 times table	Activity from *Starters and other mental activities* related to 5 times table	Activity from *Starters and other mental activities* related to 5 times table
TEACHING	**1 Tenths** *T.F. 262–263* ● Introducing one tenth of a shape	**2 Tenth of a number** *T.F. 263–265* ● Introducing one tenth of a number	**3 Thirds** *T.F. 265–266* ● Introducing one third of a shape	**4 Fifths** *T.F. 266–267* ● Introducing one fifth of a shape	Consolidation of – tenths, thirds, fifths of shapes – half, quarter and tenth of a number
PUPIL ACTIVITIES	**Pupil activities:** **1** Colouring tenths **Pupil Sheet 29** **2** Matching game **3** Missing fractions **Pupil Sheet 30** **Activity Book page 30**	**Pupil activities:** **1** Practical activity **2** Matching activity **3** Finding $\frac{1}{2}$ of, $\frac{1}{4}$ of, $\frac{1}{10}$ of **Pupil Sheet 31** **Textbook page 72**	**Pupil activities:** **1** Tri-track **Pupil Sheet 32** **Activity Book page 31** **Extension Textbook page E8**	**Pupil activities:** **1** Matching cards **2** Colour fractions **Pupil Sheet 33** **3** Recognising fractions **Pupil Sheet 34** **Activity Book page 32** **Extension Textbook page E9**	**Check-up 21** **TOPIC ASSESSMENT**
FOLLOW-UP	For **Activity Book page 30** *or* Activity from *Starters and other mental activities*	For **Textbook page 72**	For **Activity Book page 32**	For **Activity Book page 32** *or* Activity from *Starters and other mental activities*	Activity from *Starters and other mental activities*
REVIEW	*This would include:* – *key areas of concern to build into the next day's teaching* – *any organisation issues to be addressed* – *any child needing particular help.*				

Organising and using the materials

- In the summary at the beginning of each new topic in the *Teaching File* there is a list of *Resources* required for the topic.

Resources

···

General
structured number materials or interlocking cubes to represent tens and units, notation board for T and U.

Resource Sheets
14, 15, 29, 30, 31, 32, 33, 34, 35, 49

These are listed under two headings – *General* and *Resource Sheets*.

The *General* resources list the types of practical materials that are normally to be found in Year 3 classrooms. These resources should be easily accessible to the children.

The photocopiable *Resource Sheets* in the *Teaching Resource Book* that teachers may wish to use in this section of teaching are indicated. These materials are designed to be used with/by the children.

Other resources such as the necessary *Pupil Sheets*, *Check-ups*, *Topic Assessments*, *Extension* and *Home Activities* are listed in the *Contents* table for the topic and the schematic diagrams for each section.

Contents

	TEACHING FILE	TEXTBOOK	ACTIVITY BOOK	PUPIL SHEETS	ASSESSMENT	HOME ACTIVITIES	EXTENSION TEXTBOOK
Consolidation of facts to 20	120–125	17–20		12–13	CHECK-UP 7	8	
Subtracting a single digit, a multiple of 10	126–132	21–23		3, 14–16	CHECK-UP 8		
Subtracting a two-digit number	133–138	24–26		17	CHECK-UP 9	9	
Subtracting a single digit, bridging multiples of 10	139–143	27–28				10	
Subtracting a two-digit number, bridging multiples of 10	144–152	29–32		18–22	CHECK-UP 10	11	
Linking addition and subtraction, using and applying	153–156	33–36					E3

TOPIC

Teaching File, page 120
Subtraction to 100

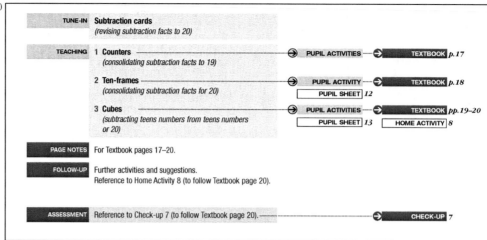

- The materials in **New Heinemann Maths** allow the teacher to structure each mathematics lesson in the three clear parts described in the National Numeracy Strategy. These are:
  - **oral work and mental calculation** using the appropriate *Tune-in*, or an activity from the *Starters and other mental activities* section of the *Teaching File*
  - **the main teaching activity** using *Teaching* and *Pupil Activities, Pupil Sheets* and appropriate pages of the *Textbook, Activity Book* or *Extension Textbook*, described and illustrated in the *Teaching File*
  - **a plenary** using further activities and suggestions, for example, from the *Follow-up* to *Textbook, Activity Book* or *Extension Textbook* pages as suggested in the *Teaching File*. The *Follow-up* section also indicates appropriate *Home Activities*.

  The teaching suggestions given in the *Teaching File* do not indicate approximate timings for each part of the lesson. Professional judgement must be used to determine the most appropriate pacing, organisation and specific activities to best meet the needs of the children and the topic. Some flexibility is needed to take account of the children's learning.

- The *Tune-in, Teaching* and *Pupil Activities* should be completed before the children attempt related *Textbook, Activity Book* or *Extension Textbook* pages.

  When the children are ready to attempt the *Textbook* or *Activity Book* page it may be necessary for the teacher to discuss some of the following:
  - what the children have to do, focusing on any concerns with language or the interpretation of instructions
  - where to find any materials they may need
  - how they should set out work or record answers
  - which questions they should complete or omit.

  Teachers, on occasion, may want to ask the children to:
  - do the examples on a *Textbook* or *Activity Book* page orally without keeping a written record
  - interpret an example in their own words
  - work in pairs or small groups with only one child recording the answers.

  Sometimes it may be appropriate to tackle a page as a class discussion with each child writing answers as they go along.

- The plenary is an important part of the lesson. During this time the teacher may wish to:
    - ask children to show and explain their work to other children
    - draw together what has been learned and, on occasion, extend the work through oral discussion
    - provide tasks for the children to complete at home to consolidate their work in class using, for example, a *Home Activity*
    - make connections to other areas of the curriculum that the children will encounter during the day.

5 Assessment

Day-by-day

Much of the assessment of children's learning of mathematics in the primary classroom is of an informal nature and happens on a daily basis. This can be done during many of the activities that children are involved in such as:
- the *Tune-in* or *Starters and other mental activities*
- the main *Teaching* activity
- the *Pupil Activities*, including games, practical activities, *Pupil Sheets*, *Textbook* or *Activity Book*
- the *Follow-up* discussion highlighting the main teaching ideas.

These provide evidence which the teacher can use to determine the level of a child's understanding of a particular mathematical idea. The evidence is gathered in a number of different ways over a period of time by:
- listening to and talking with the children (posing questions and noting responses)
- observing the children (noting individual strengths and needs)
- correcting the children's written work
- using the children's self-assessment.

However, more focused methods of assessment are also necessary.

Focused assessment

NHM 3 provides:
- *Check-ups* to assess the children's understanding of a section of work they have recently completed
- *Topic Assessments* to assess a mathematical topic
- *Round-ups* to assess the children's understanding of the range of the mathematics they have been involved in during the course of the year.

Check-ups

When the teacher wishes to use a more objective, specific task to check on the children's understanding of a particular section of teaching in mathematics, for example 'Place value, comparing and ordering', one of the *Check-ups*, can be used. These are provided in the *Assessment Book* and in photocopiable format.

A *Check-up* will normally be used after a section of work has been completed. The *Schematics* and *Contents* tables in the summary pages indicate which *Check-up* relates to a particular section of work and when it could be used.

ASSESSMENT Reference to Check-up 3 (to follow Activity Book page 17). ———➔ CHECK-UP *3*

Contents	TEACHING FILE	TEXTBOOK	ACTIVITY BOOK	PUPIL SHEETS	ASSESSMENT	HOME ACTIVITIES	EXTENSION TEXTBOOK
Counting in twos, threes, fours and fives	38–42		1–2				
The sequence to 1000	45–54		3–10	1–3	CHECK-UP 1 CHECK-UP 2	1–2	E1–E2
Counting in hundreds, tens and ones	55–57		11–13				
Place value, comparing and ordering	58–64		14–17		CHECK-UP 3	3	
Numbers halfway between, estimating and rounding	65–72		18–21				
Number names, ordinal numbers	73–78		22–23	4–5			
					TOPIC		

The teaching notes give details of the mathematics covered and the relevant *Textbook* and/or *Activity Book* pages for each *Check-up*.

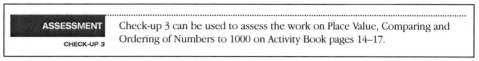

| ASSESSMENT | Check-up 3 can be used to assess the work on Place Value, Comparing and |
| CHECK-UP 3 | Ordering of Numbers to 1000 on Activity Book pages 14–17. |

These notes follow the *Page Notes* and suggestions for *Follow-up* activities.
The *Check-ups* provide a valuable record of achievement/attainment that can:
– highlight where further teaching and consolidation may be necessary
– be discussed with the child
– be used as a focus of discussion with parents
– be transferred along with other evidence to another teacher or school.

Topic Assessments

The *Assessment Book* contains 9 *Topic Assessments* which assess the work related to a specific number, money or time topic, such as *Numbers to 1000*:

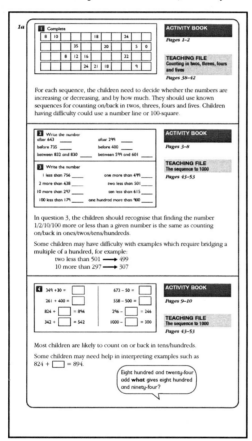

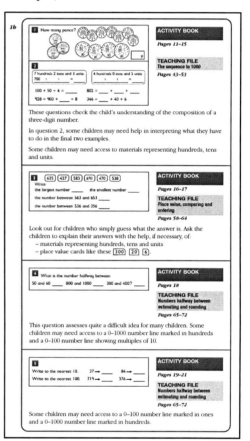

These pages are easily identified by the solid red border around the whole page. This type of assessment is normally used when a whole topic has been completed.

The *Schematic* diagram at the start of each section indicates where these assessments occur and when they could be used.

The teaching notes give details of:
– the mathematics covered and the relevant *Textbook* or *Activity Book* pages

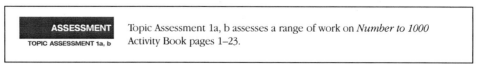

| ASSESSMENT | Topic Assessment 1a, b assesses a range of work on *Number to 1000* |
| TOPIC ASSESSMENT 1a, b | Activity Book pages 1–23. |

– specific equipment or materials required.

- what each question is assessing and any common errors children may make
- brief suggestions about how to deal with some repeated errors
- references to the appropriate section of the *Teaching File* to return to if further teaching or consolidation is required.

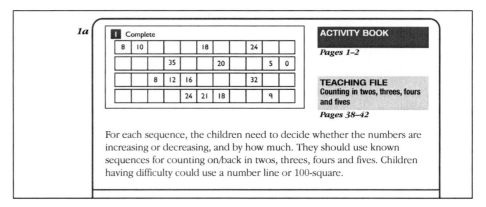

Round-up assessments

The three end-of-year *Round-up* assessments check on the full range of the mathematics covered.

These *Round-ups* are provided in the *Assessment Book*.

Round-up 1 includes questions related to Numbers to 1000, Addition to 100, Subtraction to 100, Multiplication, Division, Money, Addition to 1000, Weight, Length, Time and 2D Shape.

Round-up 2 includes questions related to Numbers to 1000, Addition to 100, Subtraction to 100, Multiplication, Division, Money, Fractions, Addition to 1000, Subtraction to 1000, Area, Time, 2D Shape and Data Handling.

Round-up 3 includes questions related to Numbers to 1000, Addition to 100, Subtraction to 100, Multiplication, Money, Fractions, Subtraction to 1000, Time, 2D Shape and Data Handling.

Completion of the *Round-ups* provides evidence of how well the children have achieved the National Numeracy Strategy *Framework for teaching mathematics* key objectives for Year 3.

Using the assessment materials

The *Check-ups*, *Topic Assessments* and *Round-ups* provide useful information on:
- an individual child's progress, noting areas of success and highlighting specific areas of difficulty
- how the class or groups of children are progressing, indicating success or common difficulties that have emerged which require attention.

For example, discussion with the children about their work on a particular *Check-up* may help to establish why specific questions proved difficult. From this discussion important teaching points may be identified.

One copy of the *Check-ups* could be used to record specific comments about common difficulties. For example, using a highlighter pen to indicate questions where a significant number of children had experienced difficulty, or by circling questions where no errors occurred.

6 Recording progress

Assessment record grid

An assessment record grid is provided on page 44 of this guide to help record class, group or individual coverage of the *Check-ups*, *Topic Assessments* and *Round-ups* completed. Ways of recording coverage might include a tick (✓) or a qualitative indicator of how well a specific assessment was completed. This could be done by shading part or all of an individual box. For example:

☐ no errors made

◪ few errors made

■ a significant number of errors made.

Key objectives class assessment grid

Page 45 provides a simple checklist of the key objectives for Year 3. Space is provided to note work which has been attempted and the quality of the performances of the individuals within the class.

This class record grid enables the teacher to monitor the progress of the whole class.

Record of work grids

Record of work grids are provided on pages 46–47 of this *Organising and Planning Guide* and on pages 46–47 of the *Activity Book*. These grids can be used to show:

– when work has been completed
– how well the work has been completed, for example by using a code as above.

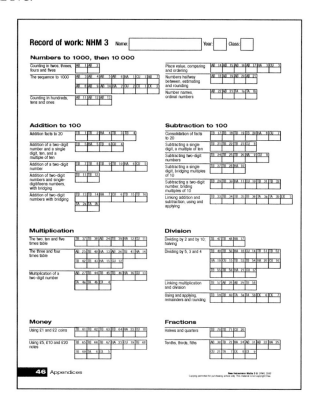

Appendix A: NHM 3 Framework planner

Unit	Framework Topic	Objectives: children will be taught to ...
1	Place value, ordering, estimating, rounding Reading numbers from scales	• Read and write whole numbers to 1000 in figures and words. • Read and begin to write the vocabulary of comparing and ordering numbers. • Say the number that is 1, 10 or 100 more or less than any given two- or three-digit number.
2–3	Understanding + and – Mental calculation strategies (+ and –)	• Extend understanding of the operations of addition and subtraction, read and begin to write the related vocabulary, and continue to recognise that addition can be done in any order. Use the +, – and = signs. • **Know by heart: all addition and subtraction facts for each number to 20.**
	Money and 'real life' problems Making decisions and checking results	• Solve word problems involving numbers in 'real life', money and measures, using one or more steps, including finding totals and giving change, and working out which coins to pay. Explain how the problem was solved. • Recognise all coins and notes. **Understand and use £. p notation** (for example, know that £3·06 is £3 and 6p).
4–6	Measure, including problems	• Read and begin to write the vocabulary related to length. Measure and compare using standard units (km, m, cm) including using a ruler to draw and measure lines to nearest half centimetre. Know the relationships between kilometres and metres, metres and centimetres. Begin to use decimal notation for metres and centimetres. • Suggest suitable units and measuring equipment to estimate or measure length. • Read scales to the nearest division (labelled or unlabelled). • Record estimates and measurements to the nearest whole or half unit (e.g. 'about 1·5 m'), or in mixed units (e.g. '3 m and 20 cm').
	Shape and Space Reasoning about shapes	• Classify and describe 3-D and 2-D shapes, including the hemi-sphere, prism, semi-circle, quadrilateral ... referring to properties such as reflective symmetry (2-D), the number or shapes of faces, the number of sides/edges and vertices, whether sides/edges are the same length, whether or not angles are right angles ... • Make and describe shapes and patterns. Relate solid shapes to pictures of them.
7	Assess and review	

Unit	Framework Topic	Objectives: children will be taught to ...
8	Counting, properties of numbers and number sequences Reasoning about numbers	• Describe and extend number sequences: count on or back in twos starting from any two-digit number, and recognise odd and even numbers to at least 100; count on in steps of 3, 4 or 5 from any small number to at least 50, then back again.
9–10	Understanding × and ÷ Mental calculation strategies (× and ÷) Money and 'real life' problems Making decisions and checking results	• Understand multiplication as repeated addition. Read and begin to write the related vocabulary. Extend understanding that multiplication can be done in any order. • **Know by heart: multiplication facts for the 2, 5 and 10 times-tables.** Begin to know the 3 and 4 times-tables. • **Understand division** as grouping (repeated subtraction) or sharing. Read and begin to write the related vocabulary. **Recognise that division is the inverse of multiplication**, and that halving is the inverse of doubling. • Derive quickly: division facts corresponding to the 2 and 10 times-tables.
11	Fractions	• **Recognise unit fractions $\frac{1}{2}$, $\frac{1}{4}$ ... and use them to find fractions of shapes and numbers.** Begin to recognise simple fractions that are several parts of a whole, such as $\frac{3}{4}$. Compare familiar fractions: for example, know that on the number line one half lies between one quarter and three quarters.
12	Understanding + and – Mental calculation strategies (+ and –)	• Use knowledge that addition can be done in any order to do mental calculations more efficiently. For example: put the larger number first and count on. • Use patterns of similar calculations. • **Subtract mentally a 'near multiple of 10' to or from a two-digit number** by subtracting 10, 20, 30 and adjusting. • Use known number facts and place value to add/subtract mentally.
	Time, including problems Making decisions, checking results	• Read and begin to write the vocabulary related to time. **Use units of time and know the relationships between them (second, minute, hour, day, week, month, year).** Use a calendar.
13	Handling data	• **Solve a given problem by organising and interpreting numerical data in simple lists, tables and graphs**, for example: simple frequency tables; bar charts – intervals labelled in ones then twos
14	Assess and review	

NHM Topic	NHM Section	Teaching File pages	Date/comments
Numbers to 1000	• **The sequence to 1000:** – uses the language: 'the number after/before/between', 'the number one or two more/less' – extends the number sequence to 1000 – introduces finding numbers 10 or 100 more/less – introduces adding/subtracting 10, 100, multiples of 10, multiples of 100.	43–54	
	• **Number names, ordinal numbers:** – introduces number names for multiples of ten and multiples of one hundred.	73–78	
Addition to 100	• **Addition facts to 20:** – revises and consolidates addition facts to 20, for example, 6 + 8, 10 + 7 – systematises addition of a single digit and a teens number not bridging 20, for example, 15 + 3, 7 + 12.	84–89	
Subtraction to 100	• **Consolidation of facts to 20:** – consolidates subtraction facts to 20.	120–125	
Money	• **Using £1 and £2 coins:** – revises work with coin collections involving 1p, 2p, 5p, 10p, 50p and £1 coins – introduces the £2 coin – deals with converting amounts in pounds and pence to pence and vice-versa – includes finding change from £1 and £2 – involves finding the difference between two amounts.	236–243	
Length	• **Length:** – introduces estimating and measuring lengths to the nearest half metre – revises measuring in metres and in centimetres and the use of the abbreviation cm – introduces measuring and drawing lengths to the nearest half centimetre – introduces measuring using a tape measure – introduces measuring in metres and centimetres, for example, 2m 30cm.	321–329	
2D Shape	• **2D Shape: making shapes:** – deals with making quadrilaterals, pentagons, hexagons and octagons using triangles, rectangles and squares – uses composite shapes to copy, continue and create patterns.	384–388	
3D Shape	• **3D Shape:** – revises recognising and naming spheres, cubes, cuboids, cones, cylinders and pyramids from pictures and by handling solids – introduces prisms – deals with properties associated with these shape – faces, edges, vertices.	376–381	

NHM Topic	NHM Section	Teaching File pages	Date/comments
Numbers to 1000	• **Counting in twos, threes, fours and fives:** – revises and extends counting in twos, threes, fours and fives – revises and extends odd and even numbers.	38–42	
Multiplication	• **The two, ten and five times tables:** – revises the two and ten times tables – consolidates the five times table.	166–171	
	• **The three and four times tables:** – introduces the 3 and 4 times tables and develops recall of relevant facts – consolidates the 2, 3, 4, 5 and 10 times tables.	172–180	
Division	• **Dividing by 2 and 10; halving:** – revises mental division by 2 and by 10 – revises linking division by 2 with halving an even number to 20.	196–199	
Fractions	• **Halves and quarters:** – revises and consolidates halves and quarters of shapes – revises finding half and quarter of a number and uses this to find three quarters of a number – introduces positioning halves on a number line and extends this to positioning quarters on a number line.	256–260	
Addition to 100	• **Addition of a two-digit number and a single digit, ten and a multiple of ten:** – revises mental addition of a two-digit number and a single digit (non-bridging examples only), for example, 35 + 4, 6 + 52 – revises addition of ten and multiples of ten to two-digit numbers, for example, 53 + 10, 20 + 60, 28 + 40.	90–95	
Subtraction to 100	• **Subtracting a single digit, a multiple of ten:** – consolidates subtracting a single digit from a two-digit number, using patterns of similar calculations, without bridging, for example, 39 − 7 – consolidates subtracting multiple of ten from a two-digit number, for example, 84 − 40 – consolidates subtracting mentally 11, 21 and 9, 19 and extends this to subtracting mentally 31, 41, … and 29, 39, …	126–132	
Time	• **Time: the calendar:** – revises months of the year – introduces the calendar.	344–346	
Data Handling	• **Frequencey tables; bar charts:** – introduces organising data using frequency tables – extends work on displaying ond interpreting vertical and horizontal bar charts to include frequency axes labelled in ones, then twos – includes the use of a computer to display data.	408–412	

Framework planner

Unit	Framework Topic	Objectives: children will be taught to ...
1	Place value, ordering, estimating, rounding Reading numbers from scales	• **Know what each digit represents** and partition three-digit numbers into a multiple of 100, a multiple of ten and ones (HTU). • **Order whole numbers to at least 1000**, and position them on a number line.
2–3	Understanding + and – Mental calculation strategies (+ and –) Money and 'real life' problems Making decisions, checking results	• Use knowledge that addition can be done in any order to do mental calculations more efficiently. For example: put the larger number first and count on partition into tens and units, then recombine (e.g. 34 + 53 = 30 + 50 + 4 + 3). • Find a small difference by counting up from the smaller to the larger number (e.g. 102 – 97). • **Add mentally a near multiple of 10 to or from a two-digit number** by adding 10, 20, 30 and adjusting. • Use known number facts and place value to add/subtract mentally. • Bridge through a multiple of 10, then adjust.
4–6	Shape and space Reasoning about shapes	• Read and begin to write the vocabulary related to position, direction and movement: for example, describe and find the position of a square on a grid of squares with the rows and columns labelled. Recognise and use the four compass directions N, S, E, W. • Make and describe right-angled turns, including turns between the four compass points. **Identify right angles** in 2-D shapes and the environment. Recognise that a straight line is equivalent to two right angles. Compare angles with a right angle.
	Measures, and time, including problems	• Read and begin to write the vocabulary related to time. **Use units of time and know the relationships between them (second, minute, hour, day, week, month, year).** Suggest suitable units to estimate or measure time. Read the time to 5 minutes on an analogue clock and a 12-hour digital clock, and use the notation 9:40. • Read and begin to write the vocabulary related to mass. Measure and compare using standard units (kg, g). Know the relationships kilograms and grams. • Suggest suitable units and measuring equipment to estimate or measure length, mass or capacity. • Read scales to the nearest division (labelled or unlabelled). Record estimates and measurements to the nearest whole or half unit (e.g. about 3.5kg), or in mixed units (e.g. 3 kg and 500 g).
7	Assess and review	

Unit	Framework Topic	Objectives: children will be taught to ...
8	Counting, properties of numbers and number sequences Reasoning about numbers	• Count larger collections by grouping them: for example, in tens, then other numbers. • Describe and extend number sequences: **count on or back in tens or hundreds, starting from any two- or three-digit number.**
9–10	Understanding + and – Mental calculation strategies (+ and –)	• Use knowledge that addition can be done in any order to do mental calculations more efficiently. For example: partition into tens and units, then recombine (e.g. 34 + 53 = 30 + 50 + 4 + 3). • Use known number facts and place value to add/subtract mentally. • Bridge through a multiple of 10, then adjust.
	Understanding × and ÷ Mental calculation strategies (× and ÷) Money and 'real life' problems Making decisions, checking results	• **Understand division** as grouping (repeated subtraction) or sharing. Read and begin to write the related vocabulary. **Recognise that division is the inverse of multiplication.** • Derive quickly: division facts corresponding to the 5 times-tables. • Say or write a division statement corresponding to a given multiplication statement.
11	Fractions	• **Recognise unit fractions such as** $\frac{1}{2}, \frac{1}{3}, \frac{1}{4}, \frac{1}{5}, \frac{1}{10}$ **and use them to find fractions of shapes and numbers.** Begin to recognise simple equivalent fractions: for example, five tenths and one half, five fifths and one whole.
12	Handling data	• **Solve a given problem by organising and interpreting numerical data in simple lists, tables and graphs,** for example: simple frequency tables; pictograms – symbol representing two units
13	Assess and review	

NHM Topic	NHM Section	Teaching File pages	Date/comments

Numbers to 1000	• **Place value, comparing and ordering:**
	– introduces place value for 3-digit numbers
	– deals with recognising:
	  – the larger/smaller number in a pair
	  – the largest/smallest number in sets of up to six
	– includes ordering up to six non-consecutive numbers, starting with the smallest/largest.
		58–64	

Addition to 1000	• **Addition of two-digit numbers:**
	– revises mentally 9 or 11 based on adding ten and adjusting and extends this strategy to adding 19, 29, 39, …
	  and 21, 31, 41, …
	– deals with adding a teens number to a two-digit number without bridging a multiple of ten, for example,
	  54 + 13, 15 + 24
	– introduces addition of 2 two-digit numbers, for example, 32 + 55, 71 + 27.
		96–102	

	• **Addition of two-digit numbers and single-digit/teens numbers, with bridging:** – introduces addition of a two-digit number and a single digit, with bridging, for example, 38 + 5, 45 + 7 – introduces addition of a two-digit number and a teens number, with bridging, for example, 54 + 18, 14 + 67.	103–107	
Subtraction to 100	• **Subtracting a two-digit number:** – consolidates subtracting a teens number from a two-digit number, for example, 76 – 14 – introduces subtracting a two-digit number from a two-digit number, for example, 88 – 23 – applies mental strategies to the subtraction of two-digit numbers.	133–138	
	• **Subtracting a single digit, bridging multiples of 10:** – revises mental subtraction of single-digit numbers 'bridging' 20, for example 24 – 8, 25 – 7 – introduces mental subtraction of single-digit numbers 'bridging' other multiples of 10, for example 45 – 6, 73 – 7.	139–143	
2D Shape	• **Position, movement and angle:** – revises turning clockwise and anti-clockwise through whole, half and quarter turns – revises and extends the work on right angles – introduces grid references – introduces the four compass directions North, South, East and West – revises moving forwards, turning left and right on a square grid introduces the abbreviations F, R and L.	389–396	
Time	• **Time: o'clock, quarter past, half past, quarter to:** – revises and consolidates 'o'clock', 'quarter past', 'half past' and quarter to' times on analogue and digital displays – involves writing these times as, for example, *quarter to 7* – introduces a 'new' notation for these times, for example, 9.00, 9.15, 9.30, 9.45 – deals with ordering 'o'clock', 'quarter past', 'half past' and 'quarter to' times given as analogue or digital displays and in the 12-hour notation – intoduces am and pm using the above times.	347–353	
	• **Time: minutes past/to the hour:** – introduces reading the time in 5 minute intervals on analogue and digital displays – deals with the distinction between times 'past' and the hour and times 'to' and the hour – consolidates the 12-hour notation by giving practice in writing times in 5 minute intervals (10 minutes to 7 → 6.50).	354–362	
Weight	• **Weight:** – revises the kilogram and half kilogram – introduces the gram – introduces the relationship 1 kg = 1000 g – deals with weighing in kilograms and half kilograms – provides estimating activities using kilograms and grams.	316–321	

NHM Topic	NHM Section	Teaching File pages	Date/comments
Numbers to 1000	• **Counting in hundreds, tens and ones:** – deals with counting in hundreds, then in tens, then in ones to 1000.	55–57	
Addition to 100	• **Addition of two-digit numbers, with bridging:** – introduces addition of two-digit numbers, with bridging, for example, 63 + 28, 35 + 47 – continues to develop informal 'jotting' methods to support mental calculation strategies – introduces a vertical recording with tens and units aligned for example, 58 + 24 → 50 + 8 – develops mental strategies for the addition of several small numbers 20 + 4 – provides opportunities for using and applying the above strategies. 70 + 12 → 82	108–113	

Subtraction to 100	• **Subtracting a two-digit number, bridging multiples of 10:**
	– introduces subtraction of two-digit numbers, bridging multiples of 10, using:
	  – number lines and 'jottings'
	  – mental calculation, for example, 54 – 16, 63 – 47
	– prepares for the introduction of a standard written method of subtracting two-digit numbers:
	  – not bridging a multiple of 10, for example 78 – 35
	  – bridging a multiple of 10, for example, 65 – 37
	– applies mental strategies to the subtraction of two-digit numbers.
		144–152	

Division	• **Dividing by 5:** – introduces mental division by 5 – reinforces the link between division and multiplication.	200–203	
	• **Dividing by 3:** – introduces mental division by 3 – reinforces the link between division and multiplication.	204–208	
	• **Dividing by 4; consolidation:** – introduces mental division by 4 – consolidates mental division by 2, 3, 4, 5 and 10 – reinforces the link between division and multiplication.	209–216	
Fractions	• **Tenths, thirds, fifths:** – introduces tenths, thirds and fifths of shapes – introduces one tenth of a number – provides extension activities which introduce one third and one fifth of a number.	261–269	
Data Handling	• **Pictograms:** – extends the work on displaying and interpreting pictograms to include pictograms with the symbol representing two units – includes further work on using a computer to display data.	413–415	

Framework planner

Unit	Framework Topic	Objectives: children will be taught to ...
1	Place value, ordering, estimating, rounding Reading numbers from scales	• Read and begin to write the vocabulary of comparing and ordering numbers, including ordinal numbers to at least 100. Compare two given three-digit numbers, say which is more or less, and give a number which lies between them. • Read and begin to write the vocabulary of estimation and approximation. Give a sensible estimate of up to about 100 objects. • Round any two-digit number to the nearest 10 and any three-digit number to the nearest 100.
2–3	Understanding + and – Mental calculation strategies (+ and –)	• Extend understanding of the operations of addition and subtraction, read and begin to write the related vocabulary, and continue to recognise that addition can be done in any order. Use the +, – and = signs. • Extend understanding that subtraction is the inverse of addition. • Say or write a subtraction statement corresponding to a given addition statement, and vice versa. • Use known number facts and place value to add/subtract mentally.
	Money and 'real life' problems Making decisions, checking results	• Solve word problems involving numbers in real life, money and measures, using one or more steps, including finding totals and giving change, and working out which coins to pay. Explain how the problem was solved. • Recognise all coins and notes. **Understand and use £.p notation** (for example, know that £3·06 is £3 and 6p).
	Mental calculation strategies (+ and –) Pencil and paper procedures	• Derive quickly: all pairs of multiples of 5 with a total of 100 (e.g. 35 + 65). • Identify near doubles, using doubles already known (e.g. 80 + 81). • Use known number facts and place value to add/subtract mentally. • Bridge through a multiple of 10, then adjust. • Use informal pencil and paper methods to support, record or explain HTU ± TU, HTU ± HTU. Begin to use column addition and subtraction for HTU ± TU where the calculation cannot easily be done mentally.
4–6	Measure, including problems	• Read and begin to write the vocabulary related to capacity. Measure and compare using standard units (l, ml). Know the relationship between litres and millilitres. • Suggest suitable units and measuring equipment to estimate or measure capacity. • Read scales to the nearest division (labelled or unlabelled). Record estimates and measurements to the nearest whole or half unit (e.g. about 3.5l), or in mixed units (e.g. 3l and 500ml).
	Shape and space Reasoning about shapes	• **Identify** and sketch **lines of symmetry in simple shapes, and recognise shapes with no lines of symmetry**. Sketch the reflection of a simple shape in a mirror line along one edge. • Classify and describe 3-D shapes, including the hemi-sphere, prism ... referring to properties such as the number or shapes of faces, the number of sides/edges and vertices, whether sides/edges are the same length ... • Make and describe shapes and patterns: for example, explore the different shapes that can be made from four cubes. Relate solid shapes to pictures of them.
7	Assess and review	

Unit	Framework Topic	Objectives: children will be taught to ...
8	Counting, properties of numbers and number sequences	• Recognise two-digit and three-digit multiples of 2, 5 or 10, and three-digit multiples of 50 and 100.
9–10	Understanding × and ÷ Mental calculation strategies (× and ÷) Money and 'real life' problems Making decisions and checking results	• **Recognise that division is the inverse of multiplication**, and that halving is the inverse of doubling. • Derive quickly: doubles of all whole numbers to at least 20 (e.g. 17 + 17 or 17 × 2); doubles of multiples of 5 to 100 (e.g. 75 × 2, 90 × 2); doubles of multiples of 50 to 500 (e.g. 450 × 2); and all the corresponding halves (e.g. 36 ÷ 2, half of 130, 900 ÷ 2). • To multiply by 10/100, shift the digits one/two places to the left. • Use doubling or halving, starting from known facts (e.g. 8 × 4 is double 4 × 4). • Say or write a division statement corresponding to a given multiplication statement. • Use known number facts and place value to carry out mentally simple multiplications and divisions. • Begin to find remainders after simple division. • Round up or down after division, depending on the context.
11	Fractions	• Recognise unit fractions such as $\frac{1}{2}, \frac{1}{3}, \frac{1}{4}, \frac{1}{5}, \frac{1}{10}$ **and use them to find fractions of shapes and numbers.** Begin to recognise simple fractions that are several parts of a whole, such as $\frac{3}{4}, \frac{2}{3}$ or $\frac{3}{10}$. Begin to recognise simple equivalent fractions: for example, five tenths and one half, five fifths and one whole. Compare familiar fractions: for example, know that on the number line one half lies between one quarter and three quarters. Estimate a simple fraction.
12	Understanding + and – Mental calculation strategies (+ and –) Pencil and paper procedures Making decisions, checking results	• Know by heart: all pairs of multiples of 100 with a total of 1000 (e.g. 300 + 700). • Find a small difference by counting up from the smaller to the larger number (e.g. 102 – 97). • **Add and subtract mentally a 'near multiple of 10' to or from a two-digit number** by adding or subtracting 10, 20, 30 and adjusting. • Use known number facts and place value to add/subtract mentally. • Bridge through a multiple of 10, then adjust. • Use informal pencil and paper methods to support, record or explain HTU ± TU, HTU ± HTU. Begin to use column addition and subtraction for HTU ± TU where the calculation cannot easily be done mentally.
13	Time, including problems	• Read and begin to write the vocabulary related to time. **Use units of time and know the relationships between them (second, minute, hour, day, week, month, year).** Suggest suitable units to estimate or measure time. Read the time to 5 minutes on an analogue clock and a 12-hour digital clock, and use the notation 9:40.
14	Handling data	• **Solve a given problem by organising and interpreting numerical data in simple lists, tables and graphs,** for example: Venn and Carroll diagrams (one criterion).
	Assess and review	

32 Appendices

New Heinemann Maths 3 © *SPMG 200*
Copying permitted for purchasing school only. This material is not copyright free

NHM Topic	NHM Section	Teaching File pages	Date/comments
Numbers to 1000	• **Numbers halfway between, estimating and rounding:** – deals with numbers halfway between two given numbers – develops ideas about estimation of a number from its position on a number line – consolidates rounding to the nearest ten and introduces rounding to the nearest hundred.	65–72	
	• **Number names, ordinal numbers:** – consolidates first, second, … tenth and the notation 1st, 2nd, … tenth – introduces eleventh, twelfth, … twentieth and the notation 11th, 12th, … 20th.	73–78	
Subtraction to 100	• **Linking addition and subtraction, using and applying:** – links addition and subtraction of two-digit numbers – uses and applies addition and subtraction of two-digit numbers – applies mental strategies to addition and subtraction of two-digit numbers.	153–156	
Money	• **Using £5, £10 and £20 notes:** – introduces £5, £10 and £20 notes – deals with counting and laying out mixed collections of coins and notes to £39.99 – includes finding change from £5 and £10 – provides opportunities for using and applying the above.	244–249	

Addition and Subtraction to 1000	• **Addition of two-digit numbers, bridging 100:**
	– extends addition doubles/near doubles to:
	  – doubles of numbers from 15 + 15 to 20 + 20
	  – doubles of multiples of 5 from 50 + 50 to 100 + 100
	– deals with mental addition of multiples of ten, bridging 100, for example, 40 + 70, 80 + 60 and mental addition of two-digit numbers and multiples of ten, bridging 100, for example, 73 + 50, 30 + 94
	– introduces addition of two-digit numbers: bridging 100, for example, 52 + 64; bridging 10 and 100, for example, 57 + 68.
		278–288	

Capacity	• **Capacity:** – revises the litre and introduces the half-litre – introduces millilitres – uses litres and millilitres in problem solving contexts.	337–341	
2D Shape	• **2D Shape: symmetry:** – deals with recognising lines of symmetry – deals with completing patterns with one or two lines of symmetry.	398–402	
3D Shape	• **3D Shape:** – revises identifying spheres, cubes, cuboids, cones, cylinders, pyramids and prisms – builds models with 3D shapes.	376–381	

NHM Topic	NHM Section	Teaching File pages	Date/comments
Multiplication	• **Multiplication of a two-digit number:** – deals with multiples of 2, 5, 10, 50 and 100		
Multiplication	• **Multiplication of a two-digit number:** – introduces multiplication of multiples of 10 up to 50 by 2, 3, 4, 5 and 10 – revises doubling to double 15 and extends this to doubling 16 to 20 – introduces multiplication of a two-digit number by 2, 3 and 4, without bridging, for example, 2 × 41, 4 × 22 – uses and applies multiplication facts.	181–188	

Division	• **Linking multiplication and division:**
	– consolidates the link between:
	  – doubling a number to 20 and halving an even number to 40
	  – doubling a multiple of 5 to 50 and halving a multiple of 10 to 100
	– introduces the link between doubling a multiple of 50 to 500 and halving a multiple of 100 to 1000
	– links multiplication and division: involving 10 and 100; involving tables facts.
		217–224	

	• **Using and applying, remainders:** – introduces remainders through grouping and sharing – deals with rounding answers in context.	225–230	
Fractions	• **Halves and quarters:** – revises and consolidates halves and quarters of shapes – revises finding half and quarter of a number and uses this to find three quarters of a number – introduces positioning halves on a number line and extends this to positioning quarters on a number lines.	256–260	
	• **Tenths, thirds, fifths:** – introduces tenths, thirds and fifths of shapes – introduces one tenth of a number – provides extension activitites which introduce one third and one fifth of a number.	261–269	
Addition and Subtraction to 1000	• **Addition involving three-digit numbers:** – deals with mental addition of a three-digit number and a single digit or 10, bridging a multiple of ten and a hundred (526 + 7, 215 + 10, 8 + 396) – extends mental addition of 9 and 11 to three-digit numbers (263 + 9, 895 + 11) – extends addition of multiples of 10 to three-digit numbers reaching but not bridging hundreds, for example, 520 + 60, 328 + 50 – introduces addition of two multiples of 100, reaching but not bridging a thousand (400 + 300, 200 + 800) – introduces addition of multiples of 100 and two-/three-digit numbers, not bridging 1000 (400 + 245, 76 + 500) – deals with addition of two- and three-digit numbers with no bridging of multiples of ten or a hundred (416 + 63, 91 + 704).	289–296	
	• **Subtraction involving three-digit numbers:** – deals with subtracting 10 from three-digit numbers, bridging a multiple of 100, for example, 302 – 10, 406 – 10, and subtracting multiples of 10 from numbers between 100 and 199, bridging 100 (117 – 60, 153 – 90) – extends subtraction of 9 and 11 to three-digit numbers, for example, 305 – 9, 463 – 11 – introduces subtraction of multiples of 100, for example, 700 – 300, 493 – 200 – deals with finding small differences between three-digit numbers, for example, 581 – 577, 403 – 398 – uses and applies mental strategies for addition and subtraction of three-digit numbers.	297–304	

Time	• **Time: durations:**
	– revises finding times 15/30 minutes, 2/3 hours before/after 'o'clock', 'half past' and 'quarter past/to' times
	– revises durations of 15/30 minutes and 2/3 hours
	– introduces finding times 5, 10, 15 … 45, 50, 55 minutes, or several hours before/after given analogue or digital times
	  – within the same hour
	  – bridging an hour
	– deals with durations of several hours, including those which bridge 12.00
	– includes problems which require children to use and apply the above.
		363–370	

Data Handling	• **Carroll and Venn diagrams:** – revises and extends work on Carroll and Venn diagrams.	416–429	

Appendix B: Topic planner

Unit	NHM Topic	NHM Section	Teaching File pages
1–4	Numbers to 1000	• **Counting in twos, threes, fours and fives:** – revises and extends counting in twos, threes, fours and fives – revises and extends odd and even numbers.	38–42
		• **The sequence to 1000:** – uses the language: 'the number after/before/between', 'the number one or two more/less' – extends the number sequence to 1000 – introduces finding numbers 10 or 100 more/less – introduces adding/subtracting 10, 100, multiples of 10, multiples of 100.	43–54
		• **Counting in hundreds, tens and ones:** – deals with counting in hundreds, then in tens, then in ones to 1000.	55–57

		• **Place value, comparing and ordering:**
		– introduces place value for 3-digit numbers
		– deals with recognising
		  – the larger/smaller number in a pair
		  – the largest/smallest number in sets of up to six.
		– includes ordering up to six non-consecutive numbers, starting with the smallest/largest.
			58–64

		• **Numbers halfway between, estimating and rounding:** – deals with numbers halfway between two given numbers – develops ideas about estimation of a number from its position on a number line – consolidates rounding to the nearest ten and introduces rounding to the nearest hundred.	65–72
		• **Number names, ordinal numbers:** – introduces number names for multiples of ten and multiples of one hundred – consolidates first second, … tenth and the notation 1st, 2nd, … 10th – introduces eleventh, twelfth, … twentieth and the notation 11th, 12th, … 20th	73–78
5	Length	• **Length:** – introduces estimating and measuring lengths to the nearest half metre – revises measuring in metres and in centimetres and the use of the abbreviation cm – introduces measuring and drawing lengths to the nearest half centimetre – introduces measuring using a tape measure – introduces measuring in metres and centimetres, for example, 2m 30cm.	321–329
6	2D Shape	• **Making shapes:** – deals with making quadrilaterals, pentagons, hexagons and octagons using triangles, rectangles and squares – uses composite shapes to copy, continue and create patterns.	384–388
		• **Position, movement and angle:** – revises turning clockwise and anticlockwise through whole, half and quarter turns – revises and extends the work on right angles – introduces grid references – introduces the four compass directions North, South, East and West – revises moving forwards, turning left and right on a square grid introduces the abbreviations F, R and L.	389–396
7	Assess and review		

Unit	NHM Topic	NHM Section	Teaching File pages
8–10	Addition to 100	• **Addition facts to 20:** – revises and consolidates addition facts to 20, for example, 6 + 8, 10 + 7 – systematises addition of a single digit and a teens number not bridging 20, for example, 15 + 3, 7 + 12.	84–89
		• **Addition of a two-digit number and a single digit, ten, and a multiple of ten:** – revises mental addition of a two-digit number and a single digit (non-bridging examples only), for example, 35 + 4, 6 + 52 – revises addition of ten and multiples of ten to two-digit numbers, for example, 53 + 10, 20 + 60, 28 + 40.	90–95
		• **Addition of two-digit numbers:** – revises adding mentally 9 or 11 based on adding ten and adjusting and extends this strategy to adding 19, 29, 39 … and 21, 31, 41 … – deals with adding a teens number to a two-digit number without bridging a multiple of ten, for example, 54 + 13, 15 + 24 – introduces addition of 2 two-digit numbers, for example, 32 + 55, 71 + 27.	96–102
		• **Addition of two-digit numbers and single-digit/teens numbers, with bridging:** – introduces addition of a two-digit number and a single digit with bridging for example, 38 + 5, 45 + 7 – introduces addition of a two-digit number and a teens number, with bridging for example 54 + 18, 14 + 67.	103–107
		• **Addition of two-digit numbers, with bridging:** – introduces addition of two-digit numbers, with bridging, for example, 63 + 28, 35 + 47 – continues to develop informal 'jotting' methods to support mental calculation strategies – introduces a vertical recording with tens and units aligned for example, 58 + 24 → 50 + 8 – develops mental strategies for the addition of several small numbers 20 + 4 – provides opportunities for using and applying the above methods. 70 + 12 → 82	108–113
11	Money	• **Using £1 and £2 coins:** – revises work with coin collections involving 1p, 2p, 5p, 10p, 50p and £1 coins – introduces the £2 coin – deals with converting amounts in pounds and pence to pence and vice-versa – includes finding change from £1 and £2 – involves finding the difference between two amounts.	236–243
12	Time	• **Time: the calendar:** – revises months of the year – introduces the calendar.	344–346
		• **Time: o'clock, quarter past, half past, quarter to:** – revises and consolidates 'o'clock', 'quarter past', 'half past' and 'quarter to' times on analogue and digital displays – involves writing these times as, for example, *quarter to 7* – introduces a 'new' notation for these times, for example, 9.00, 9.15, 9.30, 9.45 – deals with ordering 'o'clock', 'quarter past', 'half past' and 'quarter to' times given as analogue or digital displays and in the 12-hour notation – introduces am and pm using the above times.	347–353
13	Data Handling	• **Bar charts** – introduces organising data using frequency tables. – extends work on displaying and interpreting vertical and horizontal bar charts to include frequencey axes labelled in ones,. then twos – includes the use of a computer to display data.	408–412
14	Assess and review		

New Heinemann Maths 3 © SPMG 200

Framework Topic	Objectives: children will be taught to ...	Date/comments
Counting, properties of numbers and number sequences	• Count larger collections by grouping them: for example, in tens, then other numbers. • Describe and extend number sequences: **count on or back in tens or hundreds, starting from any two- or three-digit number;** count on or back in twos starting from any two-digit number, and recognise odd and even numbers to at least 100; count on in steps of 3, 4 or 5 from any small number to at least 50, then back again.	
Place value and ordering	• **Read and write whole numbers to at least 1000** in figures and words. • **Know what each digit represents,** and partition three-digit numbers into a multiple of 100, a multiple of ten and ones (HTU). • Read and begin to write the vocabulary of comparing and ordering numbers, including ordinal numbers to at least 100. Compare two given three-digit numbers, say which is more or less, and give a number which lies between them. • Say the number that is 1, 10 or 100 more or less than any given two- or three-digit number. • **Order whole numbers to at least 1000,** and position them on a number line.	
Estimating and rounding	• Read and begin to write the vocabulary of estimation and approximation. Give a sensible estimate of up to about 100 objects. • Round any two-digit number to the nearest 10 and any three-digit number to the nearest 100. • Solve mathematical problems or puzzles, recognise simple patterns and relationships, generalise and predict. Suggest extensions by asking 'What if...?' • Investigate a general statement about familiar numbers by finding examples that satisfy it. • **Explain methods and reasoning** orally and, where appropriate, in writing.	
Measures, including problems	• Read and begin to write the vocabulary related to length. • Measure and compare using standard units (km, m, cm), including using a ruler to draw and measure lines to the nearest half centimetre. Know the relationships between kilometres and metres, metres and centimetres. • Begin to use decimal notation for metres and centimetres. • Suggest suitable units and measuring equipment to estimate or measure length. • Read scales to the nearest division (labelled or unlabelled). Record estimates and measurements to the nearest whole or half unit (e.g. 'about 1·5 m'), or in mixed units (e.g. '3 m and 20 cm').	
Shape and space Reasoning about shapes	• Classify and describe 2-D shapes, including the semi-circle, quadrilateral ... referring to properties such as reflective symmetry (2-D), the number or shapes of faces, the number of sides/edges and vertices, whether sides/edges are the same length, whether or not angles are right angles ... • Make and describe shapes and patterns: for example, explore the different shapes that can be made from four cubes. Relate solid shapes to pictures of them. • Read and begin to write the vocabulary related to position, direction and movement: for example, describe and find the position of a square on a grid of squares with the rows and columns labelled. Recognise and use the four compass directions N, S, E, W. • Make and describe right-angled turns, including turns between the four compass points. **Identify right angles** in 2-D shapes and the environment. Recognise that a straight line is equivalent to two right angles. Compare angles with a right angle.	
Assess and review		

Framework Topic	Objectives: children will be taught to ...	Date/comments
Understanding + and –	• Extend understanding of the operations of addition and subtraction, read and begin to write the related vocabulary, and continue to recognise that addition can be done in any order. Use the +, – and = signs. • Extend understanding that subtraction is the inverse of addition.	
Mental calculations strategies (+ and –)	• **Know by heart: all addition and subtraction facts for each number to 20;** • Use knowledge that addition can be done in any order to do mental calculations more efficiently. For example: put the larger number first and count on; partition into '5 and a bit' when adding 6, 7, 8 or 9 (e.g. 47 + 8 = 45 + 2 + 5 + 3 = 50 + 5 = 55); partition into tens and units, then recombine (e.g. 34 + 53 = 30 + 50 + 4 + 3). • **Add mentally a 'near multiple of 10' to or from a two-digit number** by adding 10, 20, 30 and adjusting. • Use patterns of similar calculations. • Say or write a subtraction statement corresponding to a given addition statement, and vice versa. • Use known number facts and place value to add/subtract mentally. • Bridge through a multiple of 10, then adjust.	
Making decisions and checking results	• **Choose and use appropriate operations to solve word problems,** and appropriate ways of calculating: mental, mental with jottings, pencil and paper. • Repeat addition in a different order. • Check with an equivalent calculation.	
Problems involving 'real life', money and measures	• Solve word problems involving numbers in 'real life', money and measures, using one or more steps, including finding totals and giving change, and working out which coins to pay. Explain how the problem was solved. • Recognise all coins and notes. **Understand and use £.p notation** (for example, know that £3·06 is £3 and 6p).	
Measures and time, including problems	• Read and begin to write the vocabulary related to time. **Use units of time and know the relationships between them (second, minute, hour, day, week, month, year).** Suggest suitable units to estimate or measure time. Use a calendar. Read the time to 5 minutes on an analogue clock and a 12-hour digital clock, and use the notation 9:40.	
Handling data	• **Solve a given problem by organising and interpreting numerical data in simple lists, tables and graphs,** for example: simple frequency tables; bar charts labelled in ones then twos.	
Assess and review		

Topic planner

Unit	NHM Topic	NHM Section	Teaching File pages
1–4	Subtraction to 100	• **Consolidation of facts to 20:** – consolidates subtraction facts to 20.	120–125

		• **Subtracting a single digit, a multiple of ten:**
		  – consolidates subtracting a single digit from a two-digit number, using patterns of similar calculations, without bridging, for example 39 – 7
		  – consolidates subtracting a multiple of ten from a two-digit number, for example 84 – 40
		  – consolidates subtracting mentally 11, 21 and 9, 19 and extends this to subtracting mentally 31, 41, ... and 29, 39, ...
			126–132

		• **Subtracting a two-digit number:**
		  – consolidates subtracting a teens number from a two-digit number, for example, 76 – 14
		  – introduces subtracting a two-digit number from a two-digit number, for example, 88–23
		  – applies mental strategies to the subtraction of two-digit numbers.
			133–138

		• **Subtracting a single digit, bridging multiples of 10:**
		  – revises mental subtraction of single-digit numbers 'bridging' 20, for example 24 – 8, 25 – 7
		  – introduces mental subtraction of single-digit numbers 'bridging' other multiples of 10, for example, 45 – 6, 73 – 7.
			139–143

		• **Subtracting a two-digit number, bridging multiples of 10:**
		  – introduces subtraction of two-digit numbers bridging multiples of 10, using
		    – number lines and 'jottings'
		    – mental calculation, for example, 54 – 16, 63 – 47
		  – prepares for the introduction of a standard written method of subtracting two-digit numbers
		    – not bridging a multiple of 10, for example 78 – 35
		    – bridging a multiple of 10, for example 65 – 37
		  – applies mental strategies to the subtraction of two-digit numbers.
			144–152

		• **Linking addition and subtraction, using and applying:**
		  – links addition and subtraction of two-digit numbers
		  – uses and applies addition and subtraction of two-digit numbers
		  – applies mental strategies to addition and subtraction of two-digit numbers.
			153–156

5	Time	• **Time: minutes past/to the hour:**
		  – introduces reading the time in 5 minute intervals on analogue and digital displays
		  – deals with the distinction between times 'past' the hour and times 'to' the hour
		  – consolidates the 12-hour notation by giving practice in writing times in 5 minute intervals (10 minutes to 7 → 6.50).
			354–362

		• **Time: durations:**
		  – revises finding times 15/30 minutes, 2/3 hours before/after 'o'clock', 'half past', and quarter past/to' times
		  – revises durations of 15/30 minutes and 2/3 hours
		  – introduces finding times 5, 10, 15 ... 45, 50, 55 minutes, or several hours before/after given analogue or digital times
		  – introduces finding durations in multiples of 5 minutes between given analogue or digital times
		    – within the same hour
		    – bridging an hour
		  – deals with durations of several hours, including those which bridge 12.00
		  – includes problems which require children to use and apply the above.
			363–370

6	Weight	• **Weight:**
		  – revises the kilogram and half kilogram
		  – introduces the gram
		  – introduces the relationship 1kg = 1000g
		  – deals with weighing in kilograms and half kilograms
		  – provides estimating activities using kilograms and grams.
			316–321

7	Assess and review		

8–10	Multiplication	• **The two, ten and five times tables:**
		  – revises the two and ten times tables
		  – consolidates the five times table.
			166–171

		• **The three and four times tables:**
		  – introduces the 3 and 4 times tables and develops recall of relevant facts.
		  – consolidates the 2, 3, 4, 5 and 10 times tables.
			172–180

		• **Multiplication of a two-digit number:**
		  – deals with multiples of 2, 5, 10, 50 and 100
		  – introduces multiplication of multiples of 10 up to 50 by 2, 3, 4, 5 and 10
		  – revises doubling to double 15 and extends this to doubling 16 to 20
		  – introduces multiplication of a two-digit number by 2, 3 and 4, without bridging, for example, 2 x 41, 4 x 22
		  – uses and apples multiplication facts.
			181–188

11	Fractions	• **Halves and quarters:**
		  – revises and consolidates halves and quarters of shapes
		  – revises finding half and quarter of a number and uses this to find three quarters of a number
		  – introduces positioning halves on a number line and extends this to positioning quarters on a number line.
			256–260

		• **Tenths, thirds, fifths:**
		  – introduces tenths, thirds and fifths of shapes
		  – introduces one tenth of a number
		  – provides extension activities which introduce one third and one fifth of a number.
			261–269

12	Data Handling	• **Pictograms**
		  – extends the work on displaying and interpreting pictograms to include pictograms with the symbol representing two units
		  – includes further work on using a computer to display data.
			413–415

13	Assess and review		

New Heinemann Maths 3 © SPMG 200

Framework Topic	Objectives: children will be taught to …	Date/comments
Understanding + and – Mental calculations strategies (+ and –) Making decisions and checking results	• Extend understanding of the operations of addition and subtraction, read and begin to write the related vocabulary, and continue to recognise that addition can be done in any order. Use the +, – and = signs. • Extend understanding that subtraction is the inverse of addition. • **Know by heart:** **all addition and subtraction facts for each number to 20;** • Find a small difference by counting up from the smaller to the larger number. • **Subtract mentally a 'near multiple of 10' to or from a two-digit number** by subtracting 10, 20, 30 and adjusting. • Use patterns of similar calculations. • Say or write a subtraction statement corresponding to a given addition statement, and vice versa. • Use known number facts and place value to add/subtract mentally. • Bridge through a multiple of 10, then adjust. • **Choose and use appropriate operations to solve word problems,** and appropriate ways of calculating: mental, mental with jottings, pencil and paper. • Check subtraction with addition. • Check with an equivalent calculation.	
Measures, and time, including problems	• Read and begin to write the vocabulary related to time. **Use units of time and know the relationships between them (second, minute, hour, day, week, month, year).** Suggest suitable units to estimate or measure time. Read the time to 5 minutes on an analogue clock and a 12-hour digital clock, and use the notation 9:40.	
Measures, including problems	• Read and begin to write the vocabulary related to mass. Measure and compare using standard units (kg, g). Know the relationships kilograms and grams. • Suggest suitable units and measuring equipment to estimate or measure length, mass or capacity. • Read scales to the nearest division (labelled or unlabelled). Record estimates and measurements to the nearest whole or half unit (e.g. about 3.5 kg), or in mixed units (e.g. 3 kg and 500 g).	

Framework Topic	Objectives: children will be taught to …	Date/comments
Understanding + and – Mental calculation strategies (+ and –) Counting, properties of numbers and number sequences Making decisions and checking results	• Understand multiplication as repeated addition. Read and begin to write the related vocabulary. Extend understanding that multiplication can be done in any order. • **Know by heart:** **multiplication facts for the 2, 5 and 10 times-tables.** Begin to know the 3 and 4 times-tables. • Derive quickly: doubles of all whole numbers to at least 20 (e.g. 17 + 17 or 17 × 2); doubles of multiples of 5 to 100 (e.g. 75 × 2, 90 × 2); doubles of multiples of 50 to 500 (e.g. 450 × 2); and all the corresponding halves (e.g. 36 ÷ 2, half of 130, 900 ÷ 2). • To multiply by 10/100, shift the digits one/two places to the left. Use doubling or halving, starting from known facts (e.g. 8 × 4 is double 4 × 4). • Use known number facts and place value to carry out mentally simple multiplications and divisions. • Recognise two-digit and three-digit multiples of 2, 5 or 10, and three-digit multiples of 50 and 100. • **Choose and use appropriate operations (including multiplication and division) to solve word problems,** and appropriate ways of calculating: mental, mental with jottings, pencil and paper. • Repeat multiplication in a different order. • Check with an equivalent calculation.	
Fractions	• **Recognise unit fractions such as $\frac{1}{2}, \frac{1}{3}, \frac{1}{4}, \frac{1}{5}, \frac{1}{10}$ and use them to find fractions of shapes and numbers.** Begin to recognise simple fractions that are several parts of a whole, such as $\frac{3}{4}, \frac{2}{3}$ or $\frac{3}{10}$. Begin to recognise simple equivalent fractions: for example, five tenths and one half, five fifths and one whole. Compare familiar fractions: for example, know that on the number line one half lies between one quarter and three quarters. Estimate a simple fraction.	
Handling data	• **Solve a given problem by organising and interpreting numerical data in simple lists, tables and graphs,** for example: simple frequency tables; pictograms – symbol representing two units.	
Assess and review		

Topic planner

Unit	NHM Topic	NHM Section	Teaching File pages
1–4	Division	• **Dividing by 2 and 10; halving:** – revises mental division by 2 and by 10 – revises linking division by 2 with halving an even number to 20.	196–199
		• **Dividing by 5:** – introduces mental division by 5 – reinforces the link between division and multiplication.	200–203
		• **Dividing by 3:** – introduces mental division by 3 – reinforces the link between division and multiplication.	204–208
		• **Dividing by 4; consolidation:** – introduces mental division by 4 – consolidates mental division by 2, 3, 4, 5 and 10 – reinforces the link between division and multiplication.	209–216
		• **Linking multiplication and division:** – consolidates the link between: – doubling a number to 20 and halving an even number to 40 – doubling a multiple of 5 to 50 and halving a multiple of 10 to 100 – introduces the link between doubling a multiple of 50 to 500 and halving a multiple of 100 to 1000 – links multiplication and division: – involving 10 and 100 – involving tables facts.	217–224
		• **Using and applying, remainders:** – introduces remainders through grouping and sharing – deals with rounding answers in context.	225–230
5	Money	• **Using £5, £10 and £20 notes:** – introduces £5, £10 and £20 notes – deals with counting and laying out mixed collections of coins and notes to £39·99 – includes finding change from £5 and £10 – provides opportunities for using and applying the above.	244–249
6	3D Shape	• **3D Shape:** – revises recognising and naming spheres, cubes, cuboids, cones, cylinders and pyramids from pictures and by handling solids – introduces prisms – deals with properties associated with these shapes – faces, edges, vertices – builds models with 3D shapes.	376–381
7	Assess and review		

Unit	NHM Topic	NHM Section	Teaching File pages
8–10	Addition and Subtraction to 1000	• **Addition of two-digit numbers, bridging 100:** – extends addition doubles/near doubles to – doubles of numbers from 15 + 15 to 20 + 20 – doubles of multiples of 5 from 50 + 50 to 100 + 100 – deals with mental addition of multiples of ten, bridging 100, for example, 40 + 70 and 80 + 60 and mental addition of two-digit numbers and multiples of ten, bridging 100, for example, 73 + 50, 30 + 94 – introduces addition of two-digit numbers – bridging 100, for example 52 + 64 – bridging 10 and 100, for example 57 + 68.	278–288
		• **Addition involving three-digit numbers:** – deals with mental addition of a three-digit number and a single digit or 10, bridging a multiple of ten and a hundred (526 + 7, 215 + 10, 8 + 396) – extends mental addition of 9 and 11 to three-digit numbers (263 + 9, 895 + 11) – extends addition of multiples of 10 to three-digit numbers reaching but not bridging hundreds, for example 520 + 60. 328 + 50 – introduces addition of two multiples of 100, reaching but not bridging a thousand (400 + 300, 200 + 800) – introduces addition of multiples of 100 and two-/three-digit numbers, not bridging 1000 (400 + 245, 76 + 500) – deals with addition of two- and three-digit numbers with no bridging of multiples of ten or a hundred (416 + 63, 91 + 704)	289–296
		• **Subtraction involving three-digit numbers:** – deals with subtraction of 10 from three-digit numbers, bridging a multiple of 100, for example, 302 – 10, 406 – 10, and subtracting multiples of 10 from numbers between 100 and 199, bridging 100, for example, 117 – 60, 153 – 90 – extends subtraction of 9 and 11 to three-digit numbers, for example, 305 – 9, 463 – 11 – introduces subtraction of multiples of 100, for example, 700 – 300, 493 – 200 – deals with finding small differences between three-digit numbers, for example 581 – 577, 403 – 398 – uses and applies mental strategies for addition and subtraction of three-digit numbers.	297–304
11	Capacity	• **Capacity: the half-litre, millilitres: using and applying:** – revises the litre and introduces the half-litre – introduces millilitres – uses litres and millilitres in problem solving contexts.	337–341
12	2D Shape	• **Symmetry:** – deals with recognising lines of symmetry – deals with completing patterns with one or two lines of symmetry.	398–402
	Area	• **Area:** – introduces the concept and language of area – introduces direct comparison of areas by perception and indirect comparison by covering with non-standard units – introduces the use of congruent squares for measuring and comparing areas.	331–335
13	Data Handling	• **Carroll and Venn diagrams:** – revises and extends work on Carroll and Venn diagrams.	416–429
14	Assess and review		

Framework Topic	Objectives: children will be taught to ...	Date/comments

Understanding × and ÷
 	
Mental calculation strategies (× and ÷)
 	
Making decisions and checking results
	• **Understand division** as grouping (repeated subtraction) or sharing. Read and begin to write the related vocabulary. **Recognise that division is the inverse of multiplication,** and that halving is the inverse of doubling.
	• Begin to find remainders after simple division. Round up or down after division, depending on the context.
	• Derive quickly:
	  division facts corresponding to the 2, 5 and 10 times-tables.
	• Use doubling or halving, starting from known facts
	  (e.g. 8 × 4 is double 4 × 4).
	• Say or write a division statement corresponding to a given multiplication statement.
	• Use known number facts and place value to carry out mentally simple multiplications and divisions.
	• **Choose and use appropriate operations (including multiplication and division) to solve word problems,** and appropriate ways of calculating: mental, mental with jottings, pencil and paper.
	• Check halving with doubling and division with multiplication.
	• Check with an equivalent calculation.	

Problems involving 'real life', money and measures	• Solve word problems involving numbers in real life, money and measures, using one or more steps, including finding totals and giving change, and working out which coins to pay. Explain how the problem was solved. • Recognise all coins and notes. **Understand and use £.p notation** (for example, know that £3·06 is £3 and 6p).	
Shape and space Reasoning about shapes	• Classify and describe 3-D, including the hemi-sphere, prism... referring to properties such as the number or shapes of faces, the number of sides/edges and vertices, whether sides/edges are the same length... • Make and describe shapes and patterns: for example, explore the different shapes that can be made from four cubes. Relate solid shapes to pictures of them.	
Assess and reveiw		

Framework Topic	Objectives: children will be taught to ...	Date/comments

Understanding + and −
 	
Mental calculation strategies (+ and −)
 	
Pencil and paper procedures
 	
Making decisions and checking results
	• Extend understanding of the operations of addition and subtraction, read and begin to write the related vocabulary, and continue to recognise that addition can be done in any order.
	  Use the +, − and = signs.
	• Extend understanding that subtraction is the inverse of addition.
	  Know by heart: all pairs of multiples of 100 with a total of 1000 (e.g. 300 + 700).
	  Derive quickly:
	  all pairs of multiples of 5 with a total of 100 (e.g. 35 + 65).
	• Use knowledge that addition can be done in any order to do mental calculations more efficiently. For example:
	  put the larger number first and count on; partition into tens and units, then recombine (e.g. 34 + 53 = 30 + 50 + 4 + 3).
	• Find a small difference by counting up from the smaller to the larger number (e.g. 102 − 97).
	• Identify near doubles, using doubles already known (e.g. 80 + 81).
	• **Add and subtract mentally a 'near multiple of 10' to or from a two-digit number** by adding or subtracting 10, 20, 30 and adjusting.
	• Use patterns of similar calculations.
	• Say or write a subtraction statement corresponding to a given addition statement, and vice versa.
	• Use known number facts and place value to add/subtract mentally.
	• Bridge through a multiple of 10, then adjust.
	• Use informal pencil and paper methods to support, record or explain HTU ± TU, HTU ± HTU.
	  Begin to use column addition and subtraction for HTU ± TU where the calculation cannot easily be done mentally.
	• **Choose and use appropriate operations to solve word problems,** and appropriate ways of calculating: mental, mental with jottings, pencil and paper.
	• Check subtraction with addition.
	• Repeat addition in a different order.
	• Check with an equivalent calculation.	

Measures, including problems	• Read and begin to write the vocabulary related to capacity.
	  Measure and compare using standard units (l, ml.)
	  Know the relationship between litres and millilitres.
	• Suggest suitable units and measuring equipment to estimate or measure capacity.
	• Read scales to the nearest division (labelled or unlabelled). Record estimates and measurements to the nearest whole or half unit (e.g. 'about 3·5l'), or in mixed units (e.g. '3l and 500ml').	

Shape and space Reasoning about shapes	• **Identify** and sketch **lines of symmetry in simple shapes, and recognise shapes with no lines of symmetry.** Sketch the reflection of a simple shape in a mirror line along one edge.	
Handling data	• **Solve a given problem by organising and interpreting numerical data in simple lists, tables and graphs,** for example: Venn and Carroll diagrams (one criterion).	
Assess and reveiw		

Appendix C: Development charts

Counting and place value	Addition	Subtraction	Number Multiplication	Division	Money	Fractions
NHM 2						
Numbers to 100 – the sequence to 100 – introducing place value – comparing and ordering – counting in twos, threes, fours, fives – number between, estimating and rounding **Numbers to 1000** – the sequence to 1000 – comparing and ordering to 999	**Addition to 20** – facts to 10 – mental strategies – facts to 15 – facts to 20 **Addition to 100** – single digit to a two-digit number – multiple of 10 to a two-digit number – single digit with bridging – teens number to a two-digit number; addition of three numbers	**Numbers within 20** – facts to 10 – single digit from a teens number – facts for 11–15 – facts for 16–20 **Numbers within 100** – a single digit – tens – a single digit bridging 20 – tens and units – using and applying – with hundreds	– concept – two times table – facts for 10 and 5 – consolidation and money	– concept of sharing and grouping – by 2 and halving – by 10 – consolidation	– using 1p, 2p, 5p, 10p coins – 20p, 50p, £1 coins – counting collections greater than £1 – the notation £1.38	– halves and quarters of shapes – notation 1/2, 1/4 – half and quarter of a set – linking doubles to halves

Counting and place value	Addition	Subtraction	Multiplication	Division	Money	Fractions
NHM 3						
Numbers to 1000 – counting in twos, threes, fours, fives – the sequence to 1000 – counting in hundreds, tens, ones – place value, comparing and ordering – numbers halfway between, estimating and rounding – number names, ordinal numbers **Numbers to 10 000** – the sequence to 10 000	**Addition to 100** – facts to 20 – two-digit and a single digit, ten, and a multiple of ten – two-digit numbers – two-digit numbers and single-digit/teens numbers, with bridging – two-digit numbers, with bridging **Addition to 1000** – two-digit numbers, bridging 100 – three-digit numbers	**Subtraction to 100** – facts to 20 – single digit, a multiple of 10 – a two-digit number – a single digit, bridging multiples of 10 – a two-digit number, bridging multiples of 10 – linking addition and subtraction – using and applying **Subtraction to 1000** – three-digit numbers	**Multiplication** – two, ten and five times tables – three and four times tables – two-digit numbers	**Division** – by 2 and 10; halving – by 5 – by 3 – by 4 – consolidation – linking multiplication and division – using and applying – remainders	**Money** – using £1 and £2 coins – using £5, £10, £20 notes	**Fractions** – halves and quarters – tenths, thirds, fifths

Shape			Measure					Data Handling
	3D	2D	Length	Weight	Capacity	Area	Time	

NHM 2

3D	2D	Length	Weight	Capacity	Area	Time	Data Handling
– consolidates recognition and naming 3D shapes – introduces the pyramid – explores properties such as faces, edges and corners	– consolidates recognition and naming 2D shapes and simple properties – introduces pentagons and octagons and simple properties of sides and corners – develops shape patterns – deals with clockwise, anticlockwise and introduces the right angle – develops line symmetry	– revises non-standard units – introduces the metre – introduces the centimetre and a centimetre ruler – introduces measuring to the nearest mark	– revises non-standard units to compare weights – introduces the kilogram and the half kilogram – introduces dish scales to weigh in kilograms	– revises the use of non-standard units – introduces the litre – encourages estimation of capacities in litres – includes simple calculations involving litres		– introduces months of the year – revises o'clock and half past times on both analogue and digital displays – introduces 'quarter past' and 'quarter to' on analogue and digital displays – deals with durations of 1, 2 or 3 hours, 30 or 15 minutes	– extends earlier work on bar graphs – introduces Carroll diagrams with 2 and 4 sets – introduces Venn diagrams

	3D	2D	Length	Weight	Capacity	Area	Time	
NHM 3	– revises recognising and naming 3D shapes – introduces prisms – deals with properties such as faces, edges and vertices – builds models with 3D shapes	– making 2D shapes – uses composite shapes to copy, continue and create patterns – revises turning clockwise and anti-clockwise – revises and extends work on right angles – introduces grid references – introduces four compass directions N, S, E, W – revises moving forwards, left, right – introduces abbreviations F, R and L	– introduces estimating and measuring lengths to the nearest half metre – revises measuring in metres and centimetres – introduces measuring lengths to the nearest half centimetre – introduces measuring using a tape measure – introduces measuring in metres and centimetres, for example, 2m 30cm	– revises the kilogram and half kilogram – introduces the gram – introduces the relationship 1kg = 1000g – deals with weighing in kilograms and half kilograms – provides estimating activities using kilograms and grams	– revises the litre and introduces the half litre – introduces millilitres – uses litres and millilitres in problem solving contexts	– concept and language – non-standard units	– the calendar – o'clock, quarter past, half past, quarter to – minutes past/to the hour – durations	– frequency tables; bar charts – pictograms – Carroll diagrams – Venn diagrams

Appendix D: Assessment record grid

Year: ☐ Class: ☐

Names	Numbers to 1000			Addition to 100			Subtraction to 100				Multiplication			Division				Money		Fractions		Addition and Subtraction to 1000			Time			Topic Assessment										Round-up 1	Round-up 2	Round-up 3
	Check-up 1	Check-up 2	Check-up 3	Check-up 4	Check-up 5	Check-up 6	Check-up 7	Check-up 8	Check-up 9	Check-up 10	Check-up 11	Check-up 12	Check-up 13	Check-up 14	Check-up 15	Check-up 16	Check-up 17	Check-up 18	Check-up 19	Check-up 20	Check-up 21	Check-up 22	Check-up 23	Check-up 24	Check-up 25	Check-up 26	Check-up 27	Numbers to 1000	Addition to 100	Subtraction to 100	Multiplication	Division	Money	Fractions	Addition and Subtraction to 1000	Time			

New Heinemann Maths 3 © SPMG 2000
Copying permitted for purchasing school only. This material is not copyright free.

Appendix E: Key objectives class assessment grid

Year: ☐ Class: ☐

Names																
National Numeracy Strategy Key Objectives																
Read, write and order whole numbers to at least 1000; know what each digit represents.																
Count on or back in tens or hundreds from any two- or three-digit number.																
Recognise unit fractions such as $\frac{1}{2}$, $\frac{1}{3}$, $\frac{1}{4}$, $\frac{1}{5}$, $\frac{1}{10}$, and use them to find fractions of shapes and numbers.																
Know by heart all addition and subtraction facts for each number to 20.																
Add and subtract mentally a 'near multiple of 10' to or from a two-digit number.																
Know by heart facts for the 2, 5 and 10 multiplication tables.																
Understand division and recognise that division is the inverse of multiplication.																
Use units of time and know the relationships between them (second, minute, hour, day, week, month, year).																
Understand and use £.p notation.																
Choose and use appropriate operations (including multiplication and division) to solve word problems, explaining methods and reasoning.																
Identify right angles.																
Identify lines of symmetry in simple shapes and recognise shapes with no lines of symmetry.																
Solve a given problem by organising and interpreting numerical data in simple lists, tables and graphs.																

Record of work: NHM 3

Name: [   ] Year: [ ] Class: [ ]

Numbers to 1000, then 10 000

Counting in twos, threes, fours and fives	AB	1	AB	2								

The sequence to 1000	AB	3	AB	4	AB	5	AB	6	HA	1	CU	1	AB	7
	AB	8	AB	9	AB	10	HA	2	CU	2	EX	1	EX	2

Counting in hundreds, tens and ones	AB	11	AB	12	AB	13

Place value, comparing and ordering	AB	14	AB	15	AB	16	AB	17	HA	3	CU	3

Numbers halfway between, estimating and rounding	AB	18	AB	19	AB	20	AB	21

Number names, ordinal numbers	AB	22	AB	23	TA	1a	TA	1b

Addition to 100

Addition facts to 20	TB	1	TB	2	HA	4	TB	3	TB	4

Addition of a two-digit number and a single digit, ten, and a multiple of ten	TB	5	HA	5	TB	6	CU	4

Addition of a two-digit number	TB	7	TB	8	TB	9	TB	10	HA	6	CU	5

Addition of two-digit numbers and single-digit/teens numbers, with bridging	TB	11	TB	12

Addition of two-digit numbers with bridging	TB	13	TB	14	HA	7	CU	6	TB	15	TB	16
	TA	2a	TA	2b								

Subtraction to 100

Consolidation of facts to 20	TB	17	TB	18	TB	19	TB	20	HA	8	CU	7

Subtracting a single digit, a multiple of ten	TB	21	TB	22	TB	23	CU	8

Subtracting two-digit numbers	TB	24	TB	25	TB	26	HA	9	CU	9

Subtracting a single digit, bridging multiples of 10	TB	27	TB	28	HA	10

Subtracting a two-digit number, briding multiples of 10	TB	29	TB	30	HA	11	CU	10	TB	31	TB	32

Linking addition and subtraction, using and applying	TB	33	TB	34	TB	35	TB	36	TA	3a	TA	3b	EX

Multiplication

The two, ten and five times table	TB	37	TB	38	AB	24	TB	39	HA	12	CU	11

The three and four times table	AB	25	TB	40	HA	13	AB	26	TB	41	HA	14
	TB	42	TB	43	HA	15	CU	12				

Multiplication of a two-digit number	AB	27	TB	44	TB	45	TB	46	HA	16	CU	13
	TA	4a	TA	4b	EX	4						

Division

Dividing by 2 and by 10; halving	TB	47	TB	48	HA	17

Dividing by 5, 3 and 4	TB	49	TB	50	HA	18	CU	14	TB	51	TB	52
	HA	19	CU	15	TB	53	TB	54	HA	20	CU	16
	TB	55	TB	56	HA	21	CU	17				

Linking multiplication and division	TB	57	AB	28	AB	29	TB	58

Using and applying, remainders and rounding	TB	59	TB	60	TA	5a	TA	5b	EX	6	EX	7

Money

Using £1 and £2 coins	TB	61	TB	62	TB	63	TB	64	HA	22	CU	18

Using £5, £10 and £20 notes	TB	65	TB	66	TB	67	HA	23	CU	19	TB	68
	TB	69	TA	6	EX	5						

Fractions

Halves and quarters	TB	70	TB	71	CU	20

Tenths, thirds, fiths	AB	30	TB	72	HA	24	AB	31	AB	32	HA	25
	CU	21	TA	7	EX	8	EX	9				

Record of work: NHM 3

Name: [   ] Year: [   ] Class: [   ]

Addition and subtraction to 1000

Addition of two-digit numbers, bridging 100	TB 73	TB 74	TB 75	CU 22		

Addition involving three-digit numbers	TB 76	TB 77	AB 78	TB 79	TB 80	CU 23

Subtraction involving three-digit numbers	TB 81	TB 82	TB 83	TB 84	CU 24	TB 85	TA 8a

TA 8b	EX 10	EX 11	EX 12	EX 13	EX 14

Shape

3D shape	TB 105	TB 106	TB 107

2D shape	TB 108	AB 37	TB 111	AB 41

EX 16	EX 20	EX 21	EX 22

Position, movement and angle	AB 38	TB 109	AB 39	TB 110	AB 40

EX 17

Measure

Weight	TB 86	TB 87	TB 88

Area	TB 93	TB 94

Length	TB 89	TB 90	TB 91	TB 92

Capacity	TB 95	AB 33	TB 96

Time: the calendar	TB 97

Time: o'clock, quarter past, half past, quarter to	TB 98	TB 99	TB 100	CU 25

Time: minutes past/ to the hour	TB 101	HA 26	TB 102	AB 34	AB 35	CU 26

Time: durations	TB 103	AB 36	HA 27	CU 27	TB 104	TA 9a	TA 9b	EX 15

Data handling

Frequency tables, bar charts and pictograms	TB 112	TB 113	AB 42	TB 114	AB 43	TB 115	AB 44	AB 45

Carroll and Venn diagrams	TB 116	TB 117	EX 18	EX 19